THE NETHERLANDS:

LAND OF MY DREAMS

Ann Marie Ruby

Published in the United States of America, 2019.

ISBN-10: 0-578-54686-8

ISBN-13: 978-0-578-54686-5

This is a photo of me watching the North Sea, next to the Scheveningen Pier in the Netherlands.

DEDICATION

As I sat and watched the Puget Sound in Seattle, Washington, I thought about how all the bodies of water within this Earth flow from one land to another, connecting different countries. Do you ever wonder whether these bodies of water carry our stories and memories within them as they travel? As travelers, we try to find peace and harmony within our paths.

Historians study history as they travel through time. Philosophers, mystics, and religious scholars find wisdom through their individual journeys of life. They walk and cross land after land, seeking only peace. Traveling on feet did not deter the past travelers as we find history through their journals.

I had traveled to a faraway land within my dreams. This land felt magical and was beautiful beyond what words can express. This land is the land of tulips and windmills, where romantic stories are found within canoes traveling through the canals. This land is the Netherlands.

My journey to this land had been a blessed trip. When I shed my tears upon leaving this land, I watched the North Sea flowing by Belgium and the Netherlands. I saw how this body of water connected different lands through her chest. Different cultures are born within different parts of this sea, yet she remains the same. A traveler she is as she travels through different parts of Europe. Through her travel journey, the North Sea connects different race, color, and religion. Filled with spiritual wisdom, she blesses all of us with her tears of salty water.

We are human travelers, all trying to unite the past, present, and future through our journeys of life. The bodies of water flowing through the Earth have been there in the past and shall be there throughout the future. Without our knowledge, these bodies of water travel time and place as they sing the sweet tunes of history through the human travelers.

At Amsterdam Airport Schiphol, I waited for my flight back to the United States and shed my salty tears for the country I was leaving behind. The waters of this world, the rivers, seas, and oceans carry our salty tears within them, flowing from land to land. Similar to these bodies of water, I too fly from land to land with tears of separation within my soul.

Today, I dedicate this book to one such body of water that has connected the Netherlands, United Kingdom, Denmark, Belgium, Germany, Sweden, Norway, and France. I am blessed to be able to dedicate my book to this sacred sea, the North Sea.

THE NORTH SEA

With peace and serenity,

You travel from land to land,

Teaching all through your travel journey.

We journey to you,

In search of peace and serenity.

A dancer is born,

Watching your waves.

A singer awakens,

Listening to your tunes.

A painter takes birth,

Giving you life within a canvas.

As you had entered this sacred land,

You but have shaped the land, the water, the air, the space,

And all the children,

Into a blessed meditative soul.

Blessed sea,

I see you today through my eyes,

For you have entered my Heaven on Earth,

With your mystical body of healing water.

This land, the Netherlands, welcomes you

To take a break within your journey

And bless all within your path,

Oh the blessed mystical traveler,

THE NORTH SEA.

TABLE OF CONTENTS

MESSAGE FROM THE AUTHOR

"Messages received through the door of dreams, become a reality as one but accepts the truth and opens the door at dawn."

-Ann Marie Ruby

Walk into the land of my dreams, as I open the door for you.

LAND OF MY DREAMS

Through the sacred door of dreams,

I had found you.

In the past,

I had walked upon your chest.

Today though, we have a distance of time and space.

Same era, same century,

Yet we are apart by time and tide.

At dawn, the sun rises and awakens

All the children within your chest,

Yet within my land, the sun but sets.

You asked, knocked, and sought

Through the mystical door of dreams.

I answer your call through my pen and paper,

For you were, are, and shall always be the,

LAND OF MY DREAMS.

The Kingdom of the Netherlands is a parliamentary constitutional monarchy. The Kingdom includes the Netherlands in Western Europe, and Aruba, Sint Maarten, and Curaçao in the Caribbean. Each is a constituent sovereign state. Throughout this book, however, I will only visit the Netherlands through my words of wisdom as for me, the Netherlands is Heaven on Earth.

Life is a journey through blessings and obstacles. We walk in our individual lanes through memories we the individuals create. Within life, there is always a path either chosen for us or chosen by us. Birth is a destined journey where death is a guaranteed ending. In life, we all create our own travel journals. Some of these journals go viral and some remain within the memories of the beholders. Torn pages of these journals fly throughout the lands and at times, they end up within the hands of strangers.

I am one such stranger who had picked up some torn pages from journals spread throughout the land of miracles within my blessed dreams. These pages arrived from unknown people who had visited me through the door of miracles. They called me to a land hidden far away from me. I was introduced to a land known to all of the world as the Netherlands.

The past citizens of this land had walked with me through the dark, star-filled nights. I was a witness to their lives lived within the past. I felt I had known them as family members. When I awakened at dawn, I only had my memories from the pages of my dream diaries. I was blessed to have matched these dreams to people who had lived within this land in the past.

Life is a journey in which I chose to visit this country from my dream diaries. As I walked in the lanes of the present, I shed tears for the unknown past travelers. I know these travelers would want to see this land in the present days through my eyes.

The Netherlands is a land where there is no difference amongst race, color, religion, gender identity, or sexual orientation. This is a land where the Founding Father had fought for equality and protection of all different faiths as a birthright. I had walked with this amazing father in my dream as he had shown me an orange tree. Under this tree, children take birth and adopted children take shelter.

I was the visiting bird who flew into this land, protected by this amazing tree. Hold my hands and walk with me as you too take a journey within this magical land. Within my future, I know I shall adopt her as my land when life blesses me with this sacred gift. Until then, however, I shall write about this land and about her past, present, and future children.

Let us see how this low-lying land had won her war against water. Today, through her children, she is teaching the world how to tackle water. Blessed are the people who have crossed the oceans and landed upon this land. In union, let us find out how we the tourists or the adopted children too can call this our land.

Come walk with me and discover how history and geography shape a land. Let us meet the people, culture, places, and interesting facts about this country. A travel guide this is not, yet this book is my admiration for a faraway land. I want all the citizens of this world to see the land of my dreams through my eyes.

INTRODUCTION

"As scattered pages of my journal bind into one book, the door of wisdom is kept open for you to accept and witness the children of the orange tree. I welcome you to witness their land, the Netherlands, through my bound book."

-Ann Marie Ruby

May the glowing lighthouse guide you to the Netherlands through my book.

THE NETHERLANDS: LAND OF MY DREAMS

Within this land, water flows,

Reflecting the sparkles of hope.

Children make peace with the ravishing sea.

With sacred windmills,

They protect their land.

The canals carry travelers within canoes,

As they spread peace throughout this land.

From this land, her waters, and her air,

The message of peace becomes a tulip

Within the hands of all whom but accept her.

This land is

THE NETHERLANDS:

LAND OF MY DREAMS.

The Netherlands is sometimes referred to as Holland. Holland, however, only refers to two provinces of the Netherlands, Noord-Holland (English: North Holland) and Zuid-Holland (English: South Holland). These two provinces in the past formed one province called Holland. The name Holland spread throughout the world quickly as Amsterdam, the capital city, Den Haag (English: The

Hague), where the government sits, and the famous port of Rotterdam are all located within North and South Holland.

The country's name is not Holland. This country's name is Koninkrijk der Nederlanden (English: Kingdom of the Netherlands, or the Netherlands in short). The Netherlands is a small country located within Northwestern Europe. The country is geographically mostly flat and is commonly compared to a flat pancake. The main language is Dutch, a West Germanic language.

This Earth has different lands within her chest. All are connected through the oceans, seas, and rivers that flow from land to land, changing names as they enter a new country. Through these waters, we the travelers have traveled and united all humans. The captains of the ships have united passengers upon their respective ships along with the stories of the past, present, and future.

Walk with me through the life of the Founding Father, the current monarchy, the political parties, and how the Dutch found freedom within this land. Spirituality is my guide as I let my spiritual lighthouse guide you and me throughout the pages of this book. Turn the pages and see how the Dutch have saved their land from being devastated by the floods of Mother Nature and how the Dutch have reclaimed their land that was taken by water.

The world is not far from these citizens as they travel throughout this Earth. They become teachers for all students whom accept them to teach all their learned lessons. Let us not forget this beautiful land of tulips. The rolling flower fields bless my inner soul. Listen carefully and you will hear the sweet songs from the windmills from dawn through dusk. Travel through this land as a tourist and let me show you why you must visit her at least once in your life.

In life, we the travelers are taking a journey. This journey is not a religious pilgrimage, but a pilgrimage through the mystical land of love, joy, and peace. This journey is but a meditative pilgrimage through land, water, and air.

My yogini mind found her peace and blessings within this land when I landed upon her. May you find this land as a place to visit at least once in your lifetime. If you are unable to visit this land, may this book be your travel journey through the Netherlands.

Within my dreams, I met a historical figure who had united his country against religious differences. Today, I walk you through his country, from the past to the present, for the future generations. History teaches us through the pages as she guides us through geographical, economical, and social aspects of a country. She becomes a tour guide as she takes us through the land of the past, present, and future. Let us walk through the history of this beautiful country.

CHAPTER ONE:

FATHER OF THE FATHERLAND

"A father's blessings remain throughout time, as his legacy guides all even from the beyond."

-Ann Marie Ruby

Statue of William the Silent in The Hague, the Netherlands.

WILLIAM THE SILENT,
OF THE NETHERLANDS

Within your soul,

You carry the blessings and the burdens.

Within your hands,

Are hidden the keys to your children's future.

Within your eyes,

You have the dreams you weave for them.

Within your heart,

You carry the blessed love you had planted for them.

Within your traveled path,

You had left behind messages to guide them.

Within our life,

We find your blessings.

Within each household,

We open the door to freedom through your messages.

Within the eyes of all citizens,

Your dreams have brought hope.

Within your land, love still blossoms

Like the fields of tulips.

Within all Dutch,

Are found the happiest children on Earth.

Oh the blessed Founding Father,

Today, do you see your children,

Who do not judge against each other,

Who live with each other,

And believe in freedom and liberty

For each individual soul?

You have blessed and guided them throughout history.

Your blessed soul, even to this day, blesses all

Through your land and across the borders.

Your positive messages spread, as all but say,

Blessed soul he was, is, and shall always be,

For you are the Founding Father of the Fatherland,

WILLIAM THE SILENT,

OF THE NETHERLANDS.

---

*"I cannot approve of monarchs who want
to rule over the conscience of the people
and take away their freedom of choice
and religion."*

-William the Silent

History, the time traveling teacher, lands upon our doors from the past, for she knows we the present would need these lessons for our future. As I walked within the city of The Hague, I touched the historic buildings. The Hague has the oldest Parliament buildings that still serve their purpose today. I fell in love with this land as history, the most amazing teacher, walked me through the journey of the Netherlands from the past to the present. The Dutch history starts long before the era of William the Silent, yet throughout my book, I will only walk you from William the Silent, the independence of this country, and onward.

The Netherlands is a flat land where rainbows spread across the sky and rivers flow uniting all race, color, and religion. This kingdom has old castles and tulip fields spreading romantic tales across the land. The historic windmills sing within the air, retelling stories of famous leaders, painters, scientists, philosophers, and the famous diarist teaching all through their lives lived.

Originally, the Netherlands, Belgium, and Luxembourg formed what was known as the Seventeen Provinces, ruled by the Holy Roman Emperor Charles V in the 16th century. The land was later ruled from 1555 by his son Philip II who was King of Spain. Interestingly, King Philip II was once married to Queen Mary I of England, infamously known as "Bloody Mary."

Queen Mary I of England, still feared by people today, held mass executions of Protestants in the Tower of London. Protestants were tortured due to religious discrimination. King Philip II along with his wife Queen Mary I of England, believed in a strong Catholic Europe. They reigned during the Reformation. During the Reformation period, which extended from 1517 into the 17th century, reformers such as Martin Luther and John Calvin questioned the Catholic Church and the power of the papacy.

The Netherlands was leaning toward new ideologies forming from the Reformation. Turning toward Protestantism was something that was unbearable by King Philip II. He sent Spanish troops to the Netherlands to spread Catholicism and end Protestantism in the region. This often led to violent clashes between the Dutch and Spanish. In the Netherlands, in addition to the violent religious persecution of Protestants, the Dutch faced unjust treatment through the Spanish rule and taxation. The Dutch revolted, leading to what became the Eighty Years' War.

Willem van Oranje (English: William of Orange), also known as Willem de Zwijger (English: William the Silent), is a person I admire from history, who led the Dutch in this revolt. William the Silent was born on April 24, 1533 in the House of Nassau, as Count of Nassau-Dillenburg. He is also the ancestor of the current Dutch Royal Family. His cousin René of Châlon, Prince of Orange, had died childless in 1544. William the Silent was named the heir to all of his estates under the condition that he have a Catholic education and upbringing. Despite being a Protestant, William the Silent had the education and upbringing of a Catholic. Thus, he inherited the title, Prince of Orange.

As a humanitarian, he could not accept the persecution of others for their different beliefs. He also disagreed with monarchies placing their own choices and ways upon their subjects. William the Silent believed in religious freedom and wanted his people to be free from Spanish religious persecution. He was known to be loyal to his king, King Philip II, which led to the famous line in the Dutch national anthem *Wilhelmus*, "den Koning van Hispanje heb ik altijd geëerd," (English: "The King of Spain, I have always honored").

Supporters of King Philip II believed that William the Silent's revolt and fight for religious freedom was a betrayal to the Spanish King and to Catholicism. King Philip II offered reward money to anyone who would assassinate William the Silent. Therefore, one such supporter, Balthasar

Gérard, murdered William the Silent on July 10, 1584 in his Delft home, the Prinsenhof. William the Silent's revolt, however, was nowhere near its end and the Eighty Years' War was continued by his descendants.

Through the Act of Abjuration, the Dutch declared their independence from Spain on July 26, 1581. Since 1581, the Netherlands was known as the Republic of the Seven United Netherlands, or Dutch Republic. Spain, however, did not recognize Dutch independence until January 30, 1648 after various treaties known as the Peace of Westphalia. These treaties finally marked the end of the Eighty Years' War. The Peace of Münster treaty which was a part of the Peace of Westphalia treaties, recognized the Dutch Republic as an independent country. By this time, the Dutch already had a global presence through the Dutch Golden Age.

The Dutch Golden Age is known for famous artwork. Some of the well-known Dutch painters from this time period are Rembrandt Harmenszoon van Rijn, Johannes Vermeer, and Rachel Ruysch. The Dutch also excelled in science, biology, microbiology, astronomy, mathematics, literature, trade, and business.

The world became one home through the Dutch Golden Age. The Vereenigde Oostindische Compagnie (English: Dutch East India Company), also known as the United East India Company, was established in 1602, and became the first company to issue stock. Shares of the Dutch East India Company were sold at the first stock exchange of the world, in Amsterdam.

In 1795, when the French army invaded, the Seven United Netherlands went into the hands of the Batavian Republic. In 1806, Napoleon I of France, changed the Batavian Republic to the Kingdom of Holland and placed his brother Louis Napoleon Bonaparte as King who ruled from 1806 to 1810. The Dutch became independent again in 1813. The country became known as the United Kingdom of the Netherlands from 1815. Both Belgium and Luxembourg later separated as each became independent.

The Netherlands became a global leader. Despite being global, the country remained neutral throughout World War I. On May 10, 1940, Nazi Germany invaded the Netherlands, forcing the country to become involved in World War II. This war is recorded to have been the biggest catastrophe upon Earth created through human conflicts.

World War II in my eyes had shown the ugliest face of the human race.

The worst massacre, genocide, and the Holocaust still roam around in the memory lanes of the Earth. The death of innocent humans should never be forgotten for if we forget, then the death was in vain. Remembering these innocent humans and their sacrifice can prevent another human caused catastrophe. May the lesson taught through World War II be a lesson learned by all humans with humanity.

I pray the human torture and starvation deaths that had happened are never repeated. The hate crimes spreading all around the Earth frighten me of a World War III. I repeat and pray for this to not happen again. I have asked the Netherlands and her Prime Minister within my book *The World Hate Crisis: Through The Eyes Of A Dream Psychic*, to take a lead in ending world hate crimes.

The famous diarist, Anne Frank, had hidden in Amsterdam, the Netherlands to escape this nightmare. She had been a victim, yet her famous diary still guides us and teaches us through her wise words of wisdom. The Anne Frank Huis (English: Anne Frank House) in Amsterdam is visited by thousands of people from around the world every day. The warmth of Anne Frank welcoming us even to this day is felt within this house. Tears fall for this young child who had to take shelter from the evil and unjust predators of this world. Anne Frank shall always remain a young child trying to teach this world.

One part of history that is not spoken of much, yet reminds me how we the humans can be our worst enemies, is the witch burning period. From the mid-15th century into the 18th century, there were mass executions throughout Europe of innocent people accused of being a witch or practicing witchcraft. This hysteria and hatred spread throughout the world. Even as the witch-hunt was coming to an end in Europe, this fear was still taking lives of men and women within the United States at the end of the 17th century. One such example was during the famous Salem Witch Trials from 1692 to 1693.

People claimed that witches do not weigh anything. This is why they could fly on their broomsticks. The Heksenwaag (English: Witches' Weighhouse) in Oudewater is where people accused of being witches went to prove they do have a normal weight. Many people who were accused of being a witch found their freedom in the Netherlands.

The Netherlands is a land where the Founding Father is still to this day an example of freedom. He is a person I admire as an example of honor, dignity, and courage. I had visited Delft, the Netherlands where he had been laid to rest in the Nieuwe Kerk (English: New Church). He is a person I never met as time had not allowed me to meet this great legend. Yet I felt a connection to this man from another time period. As I walked within the New Church in Delft, I felt a warm feeling on a chilly October afternoon. I realized he was a very spiritual person who had believed in humanity.

When I visited his house, the Prinsenhof, which has been converted into a museum, I knew within this historical house for me was an example of humanity. One must visit this house to connect with the Dutch Father of the Fatherland, whom the Dutch refer to as Vader des Vaderlands.

As William the Silent lay dying, he had said, "My God have pity on my soul; my God, have pity on this poor people." This is one of the versions of his last words as translations may vary slightly but the original message remains the same. Within the New Church, there is Latin writing by his monument which translates to, "Here lies William I, Father of the Fatherland, awaiting the resurrection." The tour guide in the New Church mentioned, as William the Silent had been laid to sleep, he requested to have the two top buttons of his shirt unbuttoned, so his soul could go in peace.

Many Royal Family members to this day are being laid to rest below the New Church, with their Founding Father. Their bodies are typically embalmed as they sleep within individual coffins. All of the kings, queens, and their consorts will be interred in the crypt, however, they can choose to not be embalmed. The rest of the Royal Family members can choose their own paths, whether they want to be in the crypt or not.

The Netherlands is rich in history as throughout time, the Dutch have awakened themselves to unite the world into one home. From the Eighty Years' War to the legacy of William the Silent, to the witches trying to flee to this land for freedom, I know why even to this day, this land has the blessings of spiritual souls like myself. I must say for me, walking in this land was an amazing journey through time.

From the house of William the Silent, the Prinsenhof Museum, to the New Church in Delft, I felt like I walked through the life of William the Silent. Life is a journey where we are always being guided by the past and the present. Yes, even the future guides us at times through dreams. Today I live my life, yet as tomorrow you the future walk upon this same journey, you are being guided by me.

Today, as William the Silent has passed away, do not fear his dead body. Know all the dead only leave behind their legacies through their life journeys. The current monarch and descendant of William the Silent is King Willem-Alexander. King Willem-Alexander is married to the Argentinian born Queen Máxima.

As a Spanish-speaking immigrant herself, the Dutch Queen learned to speak the Dutch language. The Dutch King and Queen have three daughters. Their eldest daughter, Catharina-Amalia, Princess of Orange, is the heir apparent to the throne.

During my visit to the Netherlands, when I was walking on a dark night, I did not see the sidewalk and the main road were on different levels. As I would have fallen, I was saved by a gentleman who had held me out of the blue. Yes, it was the Prime Minister Mark Rutte, himself who had done this as a human with humanity. The meeting did not last long, yet I must say I felt the Prime Minister to be an old soul who walks amongst the people, for the people.

The current leading political group for the last nine years is a liberal group called Volkspartij voor Vrijheid en Democratie (English: People's Party for Freedom and Democracy), or VVD. Politics is not my genre, yet I must say this land has respectable people from different political parties including the current Prime Minister. They are all devoted to do what they believe is best for their country, while being watched over by their Founding Father who had given his life for their freedom.

This is the land of William the Silent, Father of the Fatherland. A father teaches his children to walk, talk, and tries to be there throughout their lives. Some fathers become a huge tree to protect their children even from the beyond, as each leaf and each branch is a lesson learned from his journey through life. William the Silent is one such father of the House of Orange-Nassau family tree.

Throughout history, the Netherlands has seen various leaders as the Dutch Republic, United Netherlands, Kingdom of Holland, Principality of the Netherlands, and Kingdom of the Netherlands. Currently, the head of state is

King Willem-Alexander, and the head of government is
Prime Minister Mark Rutte. A land and her people choose
the leaders to guide them. Some are born, some are chosen,
and some are elected.

Throughout time, all of them have a place in history.
Some will be remembered as a great leader and some will be
known as a great disaster. History talks throughout time. Let
us walk through Dutch history and see the names of the
Stadholders (also called Stadtholders), Kings, Queens, and
elected Prime Ministers as all of these people had, have, and
will have a place in history throughout time.

Dutch Republic (Stadholders)	
Name	**Years of Reign**
Prince Maurits	1584-1625
Prince Frederik Hendrik	1625-1647
Prince William II	1647-1650
[GAP IN STADHOLDERS]	
Stadholder-King William III	1672-1702
Prince Johan Willem Friso	After an inheritance dispute and an early death, he could not rule as Stadholder of Dutch Republic
[GAP IN STADHOLDERS]	

United Netherlands (Stadholders)

Name	Years of Reign
Prince William IV	1747-1751
Prince William V	1751-1795

Kingdom of Holland

Name	Years of Reign
King Louis I	1806-1810

Principality of the Netherlands

Name	Years of Reign
Prince Willem Frederik	1813-1815

Kingdom of the Netherlands

Name	Years of Reign
King Willem I	1815-1840
King Willem II	1840-1849
King Willem III	1849-1890
Queen Emma	Regent for husband King Willem III, November 20-23, 1890; Regent for daughter Queen Wilhelmina December 8, 1890-August 30, 1898

Queen Wilhelmina	1898-1948
Queen Juliana	1948-1980
Queen Beatrix	1980-2013
King Willem-Alexander	2013-Present

Prime Ministers of the Netherlands

Name	Term in Office	Political Party
Gerrit Schimmelpenninck	1848-1848	Independently Liberal
Jacob de Kempenaer	1848-1849	Independently Liberal
Johan Rudolph Thorbecke	1849-1853	Independently Liberal
Floris Adriaan van Hall	1853-1856	Independently Liberal
Justinus van der Brugghen	1856-1858	Independently Christian
Jan Jacob Rochussen	1858-1860	Independently Conservative
Floris Adriaan van Hall	1860-1861	Independently Liberal
Jacob van Zuylen van Nijevelt	1861-1861	Independently Liberal
Schelto van Heemstra	1861-1862	Independently Liberal
Johan Rudolph Thorbecke	1862-1866	Independently Liberal
Isaäc Dignus Fransen van de Putte	1866-1866	Independently Liberal

Julius van Zuylen van Nijevelt	1866-1868	Independently Conservative
Pieter Philip van Bosse	1868-1871	Independently Liberal
Johan Rudolph Thorbecke	1871-1872	Independently Liberal
Gerrit de Vries	1872-1874	Independently Liberal
Jan Heemskerk Abrahamszoon	1874-1877	Independently Conservative
Johannes "Jan" Kappeyne van de Coppello	1877-1879	Independently Liberal
Constantijn Theodoor "Theo" van Lynden van Sandenburg	1879-1883	Independently Anti-Revolutionary
Jan Heemskerk Abrahamszoon	1883-1888	Independently Conservative
Æneas Mackay	1888-1891	Anti-Revolutionary—ARP
Gijsbert van Tienhoven	1891-1894	Independently Liberal
Joan Röell	1894-1897	Independently Liberal
Nicolaas Gerard Pierson	1897-1901	Liberal Union
Abraham Kuyper	1901-1905	Anti-Revolutionary—ARP
Theodoor Herman "Theo" de Meester	1905-1908	Liberal Union
Theodorus "Theo" Heemskerk	1908-1913	Anti-Revolutionary—ARP

19

Pieter Cort van der Linden	1913-1918	Liberal Party
Charles Ruijs de Beerenbrouck	1918-1922, 1922-1925	Roman Catholic—RKSP (later merged into KVP)
Hendrikus Colijn	1925-1926	Anti-Revolutionary—ARP
Dirk Jan de Geer	1926-1929	Christian Historical—CHU
Charles Ruijs de Beerenbrouck	1929-1933	Roman Catholic—RKSP (later merged into KVP)
Hendrikus Colijn	1933-1935, 1935-1937, 1937-1939, 1939-1939	Anti-Revolutionary—ARP
Dirk Jan de Geer	1939-1940	Christian Historical—CHU
Pieter Sjoerds Gerbrandy	1940-1941, 1941-1945, 1945-1945	Anti-Revolutionary—ARP
Willem "Wim" Schermerhorn	1945-1946	Free Thinking Democratic—VDB until 1946, Labour—PvdA from 1946
Louis Beel	1946-1948	Catholic People's—KVP
Willem Drees	1948-1951, 1951-1952, 1952-1956, 1956-1958	Labour—PvdA
Louis Beel	1958-1959	Catholic People's—KVP
Jan de Quay	1959-1963	Catholic People's—KVP
Victor Marijnen	1963-1965	Catholic People's—KVP

Joseph "Jo" Cals	1965-1966	Catholic People's—KVP
Jelle Zijlstra	1966-1967	Anti-Revolutionary—ARP
Petrus "Piet" de Jong	1967-1971	Catholic People's—KVP
Barend Biesheuvel	1971-1972, 1972-1973	Anti-Revolutionary—ARP
Johannes "Joop" den Uyl	1973-1977	Labour—PvdA
Andreas "Dries" van Agt	1977-1981, 1981-1982, 1982-1982	Catholic People's—KVP until 1980, Christian Democratic—CDA from 1980
Ruud Lubbers	1982-1986, 1986-1989, 1989-1994	Christian Democratic—CDA
Wim Kok	1994-1998, 1998-2002	Labour—PvdA
Jan Peter Balkenende	2002-2003, 2003-2006, 2006-2007, 2007-2010	Christian Democratic—CDA
Mark Rutte	2010-2012, 2012-2017, 2017-Present	People's Party for Freedom and Democracy—VVD

The vast history of this land has taught me so much as do all historical figures and world history. This land taught me rather than dividing based on differences, let us unite and make all people feel accepted, not rejected. One of my personal favorite stories is how the Dutch had unitedly fought to reclaim their land.

They fought the waters from overtaking their land. To this day, the Dutch travel around the globe teaching others how they had overcome this obstacle. The Dutch had invented advanced hydraulic techniques such as using windmills to pump water out of lakes, and make dikes, ditches, canals, dams, and polders. The mystical North Sea has shaped the children of this land. Let us now walk through my next chapter, which I call, LAND OF WATER.

CHAPTER TWO:

LAND OF WATER

"Windmills blow as water flows through the canals. Humans and nature unite through wisdom to protect their land."

-Ann Marie Ruby

Windmills for the draining of polders.

CONQUERING THE SEA

The humans we are,

Living on the land

And sailing upon the water.

We build homes upon the lands.

We fulfill our thirst from your chest,

Oh the blessed sea.

Blessed body of water,

We love your blessings

And fear you anger.

A land and sea meet as they create love stories

For the children to witness.

The children of this kingdom

Want to live within this land

And be blessed by the waters

That flow by them.

The children want to be in peace

Within the land

And with blessings of the sea.

The children create windmills,

Lakes, polders, and dikes

To be safe and in peace,

Within the land and the sea.

Land and sea now live next to each other,

Providing for their children in peace.

This land is the Netherlands

And her children are but known to all of us as,

The Dutch who reclaimed their land by

CONQUERING THE SEA.

Flying in like a bird in the airplane, the pilot had announced we can see the Amsterdam Airport Schiphol. With excitement and butterflies in my stomach, I looked out through the window. "The land I love, I am finally here," I thought. The land looked completely flat. I could see this beautiful country had so many canals carrying water. Yet the citizens were not afraid of the water as they have won their war with water.

The North Sea flows by this land, carrying so many stories within her throughout time. One-third of this land is below sea level. The lowest point is about 22 feet, or nearly seven meters below sea level. The highest point of the land is about 1,058 feet, or around 322 meters above sea level.

The Netherlands borders Germany on the east, Belgium on the south, the North Sea on the northwest, and shares maritime boundaries in the North Sea with the United

Kingdom, Belgium, and Germany. The Netherlands means "the lowlands" in English as so much of the land is below sea level. The war against water was what the Dutch had within their hands. Certainly, the Dutch have fought this war and are teaching the world to be defensive and victorious.

Two-thirds of the Netherlands is prone to devastating floods. History has given the Dutch memories of these floods to live with. The 1953 North Sea flood, called the Watersnoodramp, is still within the minds of all Dutch citizens. The deadly event had struck the Netherlands, Belgium, Scotland, and England. During this flood, 1,836 people died in the Netherlands.

This deadly flood had taught the Dutch to unite and protect their land and their people. They created the famous Delta Works, a project that was finished in 1997. Civil engineers call the Delta Works a modern wonder of this world. Through Delta Works, the Dutch built many structures such as storm surge barriers to prevent future flooding.

The Dutch have a famous saying, "God created the Earth, but the Dutch created the Netherlands." This saying refers to how the Netherlands and her children resiliently stood up in union and fought against devastating floods. The Dutch also reclaimed land from the water. In union, they have reclaimed about 2,700 square miles, or around 7,000 square kilometers of land. This amount of land is the equivalent to around 1.7 million acres, or nearly 700,000 hectares of land.

The Dutch overcame the devastating effects of flooding by using windmills, and engineering dikes, ditches, canals, and dams. The Dutch fought the Waterwolf with their great engineering methods. The Waterwolf is not a living thing, but a nickname given to describe Haarlemmermeer (English: Haarlem's Lake) that was becoming larger and larger. Like a wolf, the water was consuming the land.

In order to defeat the Waterwolf, the Dutch built a powerful steam engine to pump water out and reclaim the land below. Museum De Cruquius (English: Cruquius Museum) in the village of Cruquius is named after the land surveyor, Nicolaus Samuel Cruquius. This famous museum still holds one of history's greatest proofs of how the Dutch reclaimed Haarlem's Lake through the world's largest steam powered engine.

Every eight minutes, around 84,535 gallons, or 320,000 liters of water were drained by this engine. Windmills, steam engines, polders, and pumps are some of what the Dutch had invented to reclaim their lands from water. This ingenuity is still an example of what we the humans all throughout this world can do if we only walk through and learn from the Dutch history.

Today, as you visit the Netherlands and enter through Amsterdam Airport Schiphol, I want you to stop and take a minute to think to yourself. Even this airport you stand upon, is under sea level. At the lowest point, the airport is approximately 11 feet, or 3.4 meters below sea level. In fact, the airport stands on top of land that was reclaimed between 1840 to 1852 from Haarlem's Lake.

The Zuiderzee Works was a project reclaiming land in the Zuiderzee, a bay that led into the North Sea. This project is another engineering wonder that began around 1919 and finished in 1986. Dikes were built blocking off areas in the water. Pumping stations, windmills, ditches, and drainage tools were used to drain water out from each blocked off area.

Seeds were dropped on the newly made polders, and as the fertile land became solid, they became habitable. The province of Flevoland formed from three manmade polders. Flevoland was the last of the twelve provinces of the Netherlands to become a province in 1986.

The Dutch have made living below sea level a reality. Throughout the globe, the Dutch have been sharing their experiences of hundreds of years fighting Mother Nature and reducing her fury. I believe this Earth is now at a stage where we need to learn these techniques and save as much of the Earth as we can.

Climate control is also an issue for which we the children of this Earth need to unite. With climate control, comes the topic of floods. By being prepared, we can prevent the extent of the calamities that may occur due to flooding.

The geography of a country influences the upbringing of her children. Each nation is an individual as she individually raises her children while adjusting to her climate and geography. The adopted children adjust to this motherland as well because they migrate to her, accept her, and take shelter and protection within her.

The floods in the Netherlands are mostly from the major bodies of water including the North Sea and three rivers that form one of the largest deltas in Europe. These three rivers are the Rijn (English: Rhine), the Schelde (English: Scheldt), and the Maas (English: Meuse). I had seen the Meuse with my own eyes. She reminded me of myself, the traveler. I take my journal around this globe to share my traveling history and the Meuse travels, crossing lands, as she carries all the stories of the citizens within her chest.

I had taken a train from The Hague to Amsterdam for a day trip to Brussels, Belgium. From Amsterdam, I traveled to Belgium on a sightseeing tour bus. While traveling to Belgium, I realized how different lands have geographical differences and that is how we differ as humans. Yet we are united through land and water.

I heard our tour guide had proudly pointed out to us at one specific spot as he said, "This is the Maas, the world's oldest river." I looked this information up on my favorite search engine Google. Yes, it is true, some claim this to be the world's oldest river. Yet some claim other rivers to be the oldest.

This river, known to most as the Meuse, travels within Western Europe and as she flows from France through Belgium through the Netherlands, she ends up in the North Sea. During the late 19th to early 20th centuries, the Meuse was separated from the Rhine. As a result, the Meuse was given a new mouth.

This was one of the biggest achievements of Dutch hydraulic engineering as it stopped flooding in a great way. The worry is that the rising sea level due to climate change could eventually bring floods back. Today, I admire and honor this country's achievements and progress in preventing floods from coming back.

For the well-being of their own people, and people around the globe, the Dutch leaders have taken their achievements and started to teach the world. The Dutch Government has taken a huge lead on climate change. This country is passionate about climate control and is working in union with the world to battle this giant catastrophe.

We all may have another crisis if we do not get involved in this fight against climate change and its effects. Dutch storm and water management can help this world fight the ravishing war with natural disasters, such as floods. Yet throughout this world, land after land, people are suffering from the waters flooding lands and destroying homes.

I have traveled through a lot of low-lying countries and have seen firsthand how the waters have taken over the lands. In some cases, even burial grounds do not exist as they are all part of the hungry rivers flowing by. Beautiful huts built are but just a memory of the past as the ravishing floods had arrived and taken all within their path.

Within the United States, I have seen Katrina, Florence, Harvey, and other storms take down houses that need to be rebuilt. In 2006, when I visited New Orleans, they still had homes that were marked with an "X." So much still had not been rebuilt.

I traveled through New Orleans and with tears, I saw how the ravishing effects of a flood can remain within the lives of all affected as a brutal scar that never leaves one's soul. This is when I knew we the humans must unite for one another. Everyone who did not have flood insurance is suffering and do not know where to go or who to ask for help.

Even those who did have flood insurance, do not want to rebuild again as the floods had taken away more than just a house. Some of us just call it fate and try to walk ahead. I have seen in countries near the Indian Ocean, families just move on and rebuild.

Henk Ovink had given an interview talking about how we can overcome these disasters on *60 Minutes*, a CBS television program. Ovink is "the world's only water ambassador, a role given to him by the Dutch Government." According to the television program, "Much of it [the Netherlands] is below sea level, yet the Dutch don't bother with flood insurance. They don't need it."

In the interview, Ovink described how "damage from hurricanes could be lessened with the help of Dutch-innovated stormwater management." Describing the disasters, Ovink said, "We can't prevent them from happening. But the impact that is caused by these disasters, we can decrease by preparing ourselves." Additionally, he stated, "It's a choice in the end. It's a human choice. We can think about that future as an opportunity or close our eyes and do nothing."

This is a man who believes we the world citizens can do something and help each other if we too look into the Dutch water management system. The Dutch are trying to guide the one world to learn from their own experiences. The Dutch Government travels all over this world and teaches others how to help themselves.

We the world must learn from their experiences. By walking through Dutch history, we realize how despite being a lowland, this country has risen above their obstacles due to flooding. I must say I had wondered why the Dutch would have this saying that they created the Netherlands.

As a traveler through this land, I have seen how we the humans can gather our God gifted talents and with the blessings of God, we can overcome our obstacles. By reclaiming land, the Dutch saved vegetation, livestock, infrastructure, and are preventing death from future natural disasters. If the geography can build the culture of a country, then I believe the Dutch citizens have shown in union, they can overcome all obstacles.

Today, they have a safe land where they are not fearful of the flood ravishing waters, where it seemed as though Mother Nature at times had no mercy. The Netherlands is one of the most tolerant nations I have seen with my own eyes. They accept all race, color, and religion, regardless of any differences amongst themselves.

I had written a prayer in which I had said, "Let us the judged not be The Judge." This prayer describes my feelings about the Dutch. Within the Netherlands, the Dutch have accepted all differences amongst the humans into one house of mercy. I know the Founding Father, William the Silent would be proud of all his children.

In 2013, UNICEF reported the Dutch children to be the happiest in this world. The United Kingdom had ranked 16th and the United States had ranked 26th within the same report. I believe the Founding Father had an enormous hand within this from the beyond.

The independence of this country, the fight against the water, and equal rights for the citizens, now reflect within the happiest children of the Earth. The future of this nation can only be positive as the Netherlands also has one of the largest economies within this world.

The Dutch are champions of flood control. They not only reclaimed land, but also sowed seeds on these reclaimed lands. Even though the land is so small, they have a huge impact on feeding the world. The Dutch are known to be agricultural food giants, as called by so many around this globe. According to 2018 World Bank data, the Dutch economy is the 18th largest in the world.

The world is an open book and this small nation is a land you should visit at least once in your lifetime if only financially you can afford to do so. From the sister port city of Rotterdam in Seattle, I watch the world's water flow as she reminds me of this faraway land which has taken my mind, body, and soul. As I watch the Puget Sound, my mind drifts away to the faraway North Sea.

The North Sea, a patient traveler, at times restless and at times calm, has taught the Dutch she is a beautiful sight. Yet the citizens unitedly had to stand up against her furies and protect their land. Like a canoe, the Netherlands, is held on to by the hands of her citizens. Water rejuvenates and vitalizes the mind, body, and soul, as she purifies all around her. Dawn shines with rays of hope within the land as her water sends the blessings through the windmills and spreads throughout the land as heavenly flowers on Earth.

I would like to gift you all with some interesting facts about the land of my dreams before I take you through the land. Let us find out how some of you can move to the Netherlands or tour this land as a tourist. Pages combined within a traveler's journal are for all the flying in guests and adopted children. Be the perfect guest or child as you walk through a culture, her transportation, food, and facts picked up throughout time. Be the traveler and keep these words within your traveler's journal. Come travel with me through the next chapter, A TRAVELER'S JOURNAL.

CHAPTER THREE:

A TRAVELER'S JOURNAL

"Flying like a bird, the traveler arrives in a land in hope to be adopted as the land but accepts the traveler for a day or night, or eternally. As the traveler adapts to her new nest, she learns all the facts about her new home."

-Ann Marie Ruby

The Netherlands, land of windmills, tulips, and bikes.

KINGDOM OF THE NETHERLANDS

Sacred birds we become as we fly near and far.

The wind brews up a storm

As rain falls with lightning and thunder.

Even amongst nature's brutal concert,

We keep flying.

Our eyes search everywhere,

Yet our mind, body, and soul are full of excitement.

The flying birds of the skies we are.

Throughout the days and throughout the nights,

We search for a home to build a nest,

Under a safe tree.

The land of flowers,

Bless the children who want to adopt you as a mother.

Bless the children who ask, seek, and knock

Upon your blessed door.

Tulips blossom here,

Spread out like a welcoming carpet.

The windmills sing sweet welcoming songs to greet all.

Within the sacred canals,

Waits the captain of the ship, the Founding Father,

As we arrive within this magical land.

41

To all, this land is known as the,
KINGDOM OF THE NETHERLANDS.

Mystical tulip fields and magical cottages were dreams I had as a child. I never related my dreams to the majestic Kingdom of the Netherlands. The canals and rivers flow through the land to give this picture a perfect setting. For years, I searched for the land of my dreams. With her magical aura, she found me. Through the mystical door of dreams, the land became alive and had knocked upon my door. I answered her call and found my Heaven on Earth.

As I had entered the Netherlands, I posted on Twitter how welcoming this country is and my personal feelings toward her and the airport. I was thrilled as I had received a comment from Schiphol Airport in response to my post, "Will you feature The Netherlands in an upcoming book or blog?" I had replied and promised within my upcoming book, I shall. Here is the book I wrote for the land of my dreams.

Vacationing in the land of my dreams was really hard as I knew my departure time would arrive. While I waited for my flight back home, I thought, "Would it ever be possible to live in this country forever?" I shed tears of separation as my heart had said, "Don't leave." I knew I had to go as life is not always fair. I wondered if I could ever return here as an immigrant, or a citizen. I thought about all of you who are missing out on these feelings and if I could take you through this land even through words of wisdom.

Personally, I have found the Dutch culture to be very open and fair. They do not unnecessarily say please or thank you which may sound rude or impolite, but they are actually very honest. They honestly will let you know the truth even if this is something you do not want to hear. This culture has proven itself through the Dutch people. The rest of us need to learn something from them. Maybe we too in the future shall find happiness within all the countries throughout this world.

The Dutch people are very punctual with their work and lifestyles. The Dutch children are given no homework or at times very little. After school, the children spend quality time with their friends and family. The Dutch fathers and mothers spend an equal amount of time with their children. This has created a happy nation and has impacted the whole society. Dutch adults have ranked amongst the top five happiest people in this world (Helliwell et al.).

While traveling to this land, do remember the Dutch are very open and welcoming. While you are a guest within a host's home, as always you must obey the host's rules and regulations. Be a kind guest and do respect the host. Let us get to know the travel requirements, transportation, food, and some interesting facts of the Netherlands.

TRAVEL REQUIREMENTS

In this photo, I am holding my passport and plane ticket before getting on a flight to the Netherlands.

The Netherlands is one of the founding members of the European Union. The Netherlands welcomes all European Union passport holders as they can easily travel between member countries. From a country outside the European Union, however, one must apply for all the required visas.

For American citizens, there is no visa requirement if traveling for 90 days to the Netherlands. Do look up all the details for any visa that you must obtain for your country. As all countries have their own share of achievements and failures, we the citizens must be happy with the land we were born in and try to make all countries throughout this world a safe place to live within. If you are trying to move to this land, I ask you to try and improve your own land with the knowledge taught to you by the great Dutch travelers. Maybe you can bring some of the Dutch culture to your land.

For the American passport holders, the Netherlands has the Dutch American Friendship Treaty (DAFT), which gives American citizens easier entrance to the Netherlands. Through this treaty, American citizens can travel and live within this country. DAFT is a treaty that was signed on March 27, 1956 as a part of Dutch and American international relations. This treaty removed many requirements needed for Americans to move to the Netherlands.

If you are wealthy and really rich, I guess it is easy to travel from country to country and live per your wish. It is because the wealthy have proved themselves as they worked to be rich or maybe were blessed to be born within a rich family. The rest of us, however, must walk and take the journey of our lives through our hard-earned ways.

For pet lovers, the Netherlands is one of the easiest places to take your pets to. I have looked into this as I have a dog. All of the pet's vaccinations must be up to date and the pet must be microchipped. As always, look into the specific requirements for your pet and safety of your pet and all others. I know traveling with a pet can be difficult as I have previously traveled with my dog in the United States. He was scared of the sounds and the unknown places. I had to get him comfortable in his carrier and make sure he had his comfort toys and treats. My dog is a small breed, so he can travel on board with me.

Although he was well-behaved, he did cry even though he had been in training with a trainer for months before his travel time. At times, some of the passengers get annoyed. We must adjust to this and know people also get annoyed at small children crying. This is something I believe we the humans should learn to deal with as young children and pets cry because they are scared and cannot voice their fears.

Personally, I love traveling with KLM Royal Dutch Airlines and Delta Air Lines as I found them to be exceptionally caring with pets and humans alike. I did not take my pet to the Netherlands but other passengers on my flight did travel with their pets. The flight attendants were really nice and understanding with the passengers and their pets. This is not an endorsement, but a fact from my personal travel diary.

One reason a lot of people like to visit the Netherlands on vacation if not moving there is the country's culture that holds no judgment against others. Personally, I have seen tourists visit Amsterdam, The Hague, and Rotterdam as these are the top three destinations visited by tourists. I would want you to travel through the whole country as only then, you would get to know the Netherlands completely, and maybe fall in love with her like I did.

While traveling through The Hague, I had asked an American who I bumped into at Yoghurt Barn in the Buitenhof, why she chose to move to the Netherlands. She told me for health insurance and education benefits for her children. Compared to the United States, health benefits in the Netherlands are much more affordable. Education costs are also affordable, but not free as a lot of people misunderstand.

The Netherlands is a sacred land where the Dutch have created a safe and blessed home for all whom were born there and all whom adopt this land as their own land. A mother and a father adopt a child as they create a family or bring the child home. Yet when it is a country, it is the child who adopts the country as his or her mother or fatherland and makes this land his or her home.

When you the individual choose a land as your home, remember to take care of your land and all of your neighbors too. If you choose a land which has a different culture than yours, then it is you who must change and adjust to your adopted country and the culture while keeping your own. We the travelers travel to different lands, always trying to learn from each other while honoring and keeping individual values intact.

Be blessed as you tour through this land through my book for yourself and for the future generations without even leaving your home. Blessed are the travelers of life as their journeys in union become a guided tour for all the future travelers of life. This is how the travelers' journals are written, entwining all differences within one home and one land, you the citizen call home.

The travelers fly into this land and take shelter under the orange tree. Under the orange tree, within the safety of blessed wings, the travelers build their nests. We the traveling birds or the traveling humans after a long journey, look for a shelter to rest our tired bodies. As we the travelers are given shelter, may we know to respect our hosts who have kindly allowed us to build a nest within their home. Respect is earned, not given. Remember this as you are traveling throughout your dreamlands.

TRANSPORTATION SYSTEM

Different modes of transportation.

Travelers take a sacred journey for meditation, leisure, or pleasure. I call these journeys a pilgrimage for the mind, body, and soul. A traveler I had become, traveling

51

through this Earth. These journeys unite my inner soul with different cultures. With these pilgrimages, I have emerged as a spiritually awakened soul.

The Netherlands had given my inner soul a different kind of awakening where I found myself revisiting this land over and over again. Traveling through this land, I realized I had no worries about transportation or renting a car. For frequent travelers traveling through the European Union countries, the Netherlands is only a ticket away from your destination. After figuring out where you would like to go in the Netherlands, take some time to research the Dutch transportation system.

The Ministry of Infrastructure and Water Management was established in 2010 and is responsible for transportation, aviation, water management, and other projects. They have done a magnificent job as an American like me was able to go and travel with ease. Public transportation throughout this country is available through train, metro, tram, light rail, ferry, and bus.

Within the time frame of your visit, you might be limited to your options if you decide to rent a car. Renting a car is always an option for all whom have to. Yet amazingly,

I did not have to rent a car. When I arrived within this country at the Amsterdam Airport Schiphol, I was greeted with love and kindness from the airport personnel, the amazing security forces, and the amazing café waiters and waitresses.

In this world, each day is a sacred and scary situation for the travelers. Yet the reception within this airport was as if I had just come home. I had asked about transportation at the airport, specifically what would be the most economical and safe. The representative introduced me to the Dutch transportation system.

I had taken the train to The Hague. The train ride was less than an hour long and was a very luxurious journey through the Dutch countryside. Since I had my backpack and a rolling suitcase, I easily had taken these aboard with me. Within the train stations are different food options even for a vegetarian like me.

I arrived at Den Haag Centraal (English: The Hague Central) in The Hague. The station crew was amazing and guided me as to where I needed to go. I was shocked as some of the crew had told me not to waste money on a cab. The places I wanted to visit were easily accessible by tram, bus, or train. Dutch citizens ride a bike, so it is very easy for people to walk or rent a bike to go around locally. The country's transportation system is built in a way so one can travel throughout the whole country without owning a car. The system is very clean and safe. You can meet and greet people traveling from all around Europe.

One of the things you should remember while using public transportation is to keep an eye out for your destination stop. The destination stops are announced in Dutch and if you are not familiar with the pronunciation, you might miss your stop. You might also miss any important announcements which are said in Dutch. One time, my bus had stopped, and we were told to take another one. The other passengers realizing I had no clue what was being announced had told me and guided me.

As a frequent traveler, I have traveled throughout this world. When I had traveled within certain parts of this world, I was told to act like a local. I was told not to show that I am a foreigner and attract attention to myself. Here within this country, I had not witnessed this fear and was easily able to communicate with the locals. I found helping hands all around me.

Always while traveling, judge for yourself before trusting anyone. I had always tried to ask for help from security personnel as they are seen everywhere. I felt safe seeking their attention as they had always guided me as needed. Even as a single woman, I had very safely traveled through this nation without any fear. This was an amazing journey for me. I also had taken cabs to see some of the old castles where public transportation does not reach. The cab drivers gave me sightseeing tours too, as they had stories to tell.

Very late one night, I was at the Scheveningen beach. As I walked into the tram, there was a huge crowd. There were two individuals, a man and a woman, who realized I was a foreigner traveling. These kindhearted souls had become like family as they made me feel like I was sitting in my living room. All had become involved in different topics and they had talked with me throughout the ride as they knew I was uncomfortable in the crowd. I still remember these strangers as my unknown friends.

As an example of how easy going this country is, you can look at their Prime Minister. The Prime Minister of this country rides his bike to and from work. The former State Secretary for Security and Justice who has retired, now drives a bus, and who knows, as you are traveling through this country, you might end up within the bus of Fredrik "Fred" Teeven.

If you are able to take a vacation and be within the Netherlands, sightseeing and traveling around is not a worry. My only problem was leaving this country behind. As I shed tears, I had written on Instagram, "En route to Seattle, will be home soon, yet I miss the Netherlands already." Schiphol Airport had written, "Have a good flight! We'll miss you too."

DUTCH FOOD

Stroopwafel and coffee.

The Netherlands is a nation which has blended different race, color, and religion within one home. King Willem-Alexander has married an Argentinian born woman. Queen Máxima has settled within this land as she has adopted this land as her own land. Love united two cultures within one home as the King and Queen are examples of united cultures.

Food has also united all different cultures within the homes of the Dutch. Different restaurants from all over the world are found all over the country. I personally found myself trying Italian, French, Thai, Indian, Indonesian, and my favorite, Starbucks. I had, however, tried to have a little bit of the authentic Dutch cuisine every day. My favorite is the vegetarian bitterballen. Here are some authentic Dutch food items:

1. **BITTERBALLEN:**
Bitterballen are similar to Dutch croquettes. As a vegetarian, I found bitterballen stuffed with cheese and jalapeños. These are deep fried balls with generally meat filling.

2. **SUIKERBROOD:**
Suikerbrood is sugar bread which is a very sweet treat.

3. **STROOPWAFEL:**

A stroopwafel is a syrup waffle. It is one of the most well-known Dutch delicacies globally. A stroopwafel includes two thin waffles cookies with syrup in between them. The stroopwafel can be found within many grocery stores in the United States too.

4. BOSSCHE BOLLEN:

Bossche Bollen are chocolate balls from Den Bosch.

5. DROP:

Drop is licorice, which is available everywhere in the Netherlands. You can grab it at any supermarket or gas station. The Dutch are known to love this treat of different flavors. You can get salty or sweet licorice. Foreigners are not used to the salty licorice, and if they eat it thinking it is sweet, they are shocked.

6. KIBBELING:

Fried fish, usually whiting or cod fish caught in the North Sea, is a popular dish in the Netherlands.

7. KAAS:

The Dutch have been making cheese for thousands of years. The Netherlands is one of the biggest cheese exporters, so while visiting, be sure to try the many different types of cheese.

8. TOMPOUCE:

This sweet pastry is also called tompoes. This treat is named after Jan Hannema, a dwarf from Friesland who performed under the name, Admiral Tom Pouce. The pastry is in the shape of a rectangle with two layers of puff pastry sheets and cream filling.

9. ERWTENSOEP:

Erwtensoep is Dutch split pea soup which tastes different from other split pea soups I have tasted around the world as the spices have a big hand with the taste of each land and culture.

10. POFFERTJES:

Dutch mini pancakes are usually topped with butter and sprinkled with powdered sugar.

11. APPELFLAPPEN:

Appelflappen are apple turnovers which are similar to apple pie. They have cooked apples inside and an extremely crispy exterior.

12. STAMPPOT:

Stamppot is made with mashed potatoes and other vegetables. The dish is normally served with sausage.

13. PATAT FRITES:

The Dutch are famous for serving fries with mayonnaise.

14. HAGELSLAG:

These come in different flavors and different colored candy sprinkles. The Dutch like to have bread with butter and hagelslag on top.

15. HOLLANDSE NIEUWE HARING:

The Dutch New Herring is a traditional dish that is very famous. The Dutch like to have the herring whole, grabbing it by the tail in the air. If you eat fish, be sure to have some outside of the Binnenhof in The Hague.

16. OLYKOEK:

Olykoek is oil cake which the Dutch make by frying balls of dough in hot oil. One widely believed story is that the Dutch brought this treat to the United States which evolved to be the doughnut we have today.

Do not forget to try out different types of Dutch bread. The variety of food is similar to our cultural differences. A dining table always unites the differences into one family. As I had dined within the Netherlands, I figured out food is different at times, but has united cultures.

Traveling throughout this world, I have realized foods are unique to each culture, yet are very similar. In the Netherlands, all the restaurants adjusted the food to my taste and to meet my dietary needs. For me, they had made vegetarian bitterballen. The world cuisines and the world travelers in union create the open kitchens in all open nations.

INTERESTING FACTS

Throughout this world, we have interesting facts about each land and culture. Through my travel journeys, I have picked up some interesting facts about the Netherlands and the Dutch. Walk with me through these interesting facts.

1. The official name is the Kingdom of the Netherlands, which includes the Netherlands, Aruba, Sint Maarten, and Curaçao.
2. The capital city is Amsterdam.
3. Cycling is popular, but bike helmets are not. Even then, bike related accidents are lowest in the world.
4. King Willem-Alexander was the first Dutch King in 123 years.
5. The official language is Dutch. The Dutch language is a West Germanic language, spoken by roughly 14 million people. In the province of Friesland, Frisian is an official language. Other regional languages also recognized include English, Limburgish, Papiamento, and Dutch Low Saxon.
6. It is said 80% of the flower bulbs in this world come from this blessed country.
7. King Willem-Alexander is married to Queen Máxima, the first foreign Dutch Queen born in Latin America.
8. There are numerous parking lots just for bikes.

9. This country has the lowest elevation in Europe, but has overcome the fears of water and flood.

10. The population of the Netherlands is around 17 million people.

11. The Hague is commonly known as the world's legal capital.

12. The currency is the euro as the Netherlands is a part of the European Union. Within the Dutch Caribbean, Aruba uses the Aruban florin, and both Sint Maarten and Curaçao use the Netherlands Antillean guilder. The U.S. dollar, however, is accepted in Aruba, Sint Maarten, and Curaçao.

13. The flag of the Netherlands has the same colors as the American flag, but originally the flag of the Netherlands was orange, blue, and white. The orange color had to be changed to red as the color dye would get darker overtime. This tricolor flag is the oldest one in the world and was used by William the Silent during the Dutch Revolt.

14. The Netherlands is mostly flat, with the highest elevation of around 1,058 feet, or 322 meters at Vaalserberg.

15. The Netherlands is the world's second biggest beer exporter.

16. The religion most people practice in the Netherlands is Protestantism, however 50% of the Dutch are non-religious.

17. Amsterdam Airport Schiphol has the most direct flights within this world. I was lucky as there are direct flights from Seattle to Amsterdam.

18. In 2001, the Netherlands had legalized same-sex marriages and was the first country in the world to do so.

19. The Dutch are advanced in the world of health and science as amongst all other achievements, they had also made the first artificial heart.

20. The Dutch national color is orange.

21. Walking through the land is very safe as the Dutch do not have any stray dogs. They give loving homes to their four-legged friends.

22. Carrots were originally black, yellow, red, purple, and white. There are stories exploring the origin of the orange carrots, linking the color back to the Dutch revolution. These stories say that in honor of the Father of the Fatherland, William the Silent, carrots were turned orange.

23. The national anthem "Het Wilhelmus," was written in the late 1560s or early 1570s. Even though this

anthem was recorded to have been written before all existing anthems, it was not declared as an anthem until 1932. Therefore, this is the oldest written anthem still in use today.

24. This small European country has mixed nationalities as one-fifth of the Dutch population is known to be descendants of foreign immigrants.

25. Giethoorn is a famous village where there are barely any streets. The primary way to travel is through the canals. This is also known as the "Venice" of the Netherlands.

26. The Dutch greet callers over the phone with their last name. So, I would say, "Ruby" not "Ann Marie."

27. The Dutch are said to have more bikes than humans.

28. The father of microbiology, Antoine Philips van Leeuwenhoek, was from Delft, the Netherlands.

29. Koninklijke Luchtvaart Maatschappij (English: KLM Royal Dutch Airlines), was founded in 1919 and is the world's oldest airline still operating today.

30. Madurodam was opened in the Netherlands on July 2, 1952. Walt Disney's inspiration after visiting this park is evident when he later opened the Storybook Land Canal Boats attraction at Disneyland on July 17, 1955.

31. Flessenlikker is a bottle licker that helps scrape out the last bit from a bottle, as the Dutch are known to be very thrifty.

32. The Dutch are the world's largest producer of tulips, yet tulips originally did not grow here. Tulips were brought here from Turkey.

33. In the Netherlands, it is normal to greet your guest with three kisses on the cheek, starting from right, to left, to right.

34. The Dutch usually do not use curtains on their windows. I had seen this when I rented an apartment for a few weeks. All the reviews had said to make sure you have curtains, as this is a common practice in the Netherlands.

35. It is illegal to ride a bike if you do not have a bell and a light.

36. According to Oxfam's Food Index, the Dutch have the healthiest diet overall in the world based on having enough to eat, affordability, food quality, and health. As a diabetic (due to genetics), I saw their healthy diet firsthand as my blood sugar was under control even without a very strict diet which I normally live with.

37. The Dutch are honest and blunt. They appreciate honesty. My tour guide had said not to get offended by their bluntness for it is their culture.

38. The Dutch have a great healthcare system which is one of the best and very affordable.

39. No homework keeps the children and parents happy. According to UNICEF, the Dutch have proven to be the happiest children in the world. We need to take a lesson from the Dutch culture and spread this happiness throughout the globe.

40. From medieval times, the Dutch have worn klompen (English: clogs or wooden shoes) to protect their feet. The wooden shoes are solid and prevent things from going in, unlike a lot of the shoes worn today. Now, this wooden shoe is mostly a souvenir found all throughout the Netherlands. I was able to buy some wooden ones during my travel. After I placed coins into a coin box at Madurodam, a small pair of blue and white clogs appeared on a miniature train. Do remember to get a pair of clogs for yourself.

41. The national dish is raw herring.

42. The world-famous Edam cheese is from the town of Edam in North Holland. You can still relive a day at the Edam cheese market from medieval times on

certain days during the summer. Be sure to check out their schedule.

43. Dutch settlers brought the olykoek (English: oil cake) to New Amsterdam, which today is known as New York. Some claim this Dutch sweet treat is the origin of the present-day doughnut.

44. Efteling is an amusement park within the province of North Brabant. This park was first opened on May 31, 1952. This park is very similar to Disneyland which was opened on July 17, 1955.

45. The Dutch eat sprinkles for breakfast on bread and other breakfast items. This is referred to as "hagelslag." This was offered to me in an all-inclusive resort I had once stayed at.

46. Christmas is celebrated in this land throughout December as the Christmas celebration starts early. The Dutch celebrate Saint Nicholas' Eve on December 5th and Saint Nicholas' Day on December 6th. I have made a lot of Dutch friends and all have told me to come back during Christmas, as they celebrate throughout the season. I would love to see the old buildings in The Hague and Amsterdam decorated during the Christmas holidays.

47. One of the most famous cheeses worldwide is Gouda cheese, named after the town where it was traded in South Holland. Records of Gouda cheese date back to 1184.

48. Throughout the world, Saint Nicholas is known as Santa Claus. This is because in Dutch, Saint Nicholas translates to Sinterklaas which has globally now turned into "Santa Claus."

49. Many Dutch people live in condos and multi-unit homes. Standalone homes or detached villas are rare, but available. The historical villas and beautiful colorful homes are magical. I would love to live in a magical Dutch home, maybe with a windmill on the property. This dream could be a reality in this country.

50. Learn to bike, as then you can travel around easily. Remember if you need to walk across the bike lanes, be careful as the cyclists do not stop. I had this problem quite a few times, when I unknowingly walked through the bike lanes.

51. In the 2019 United Nations' World Happiness Report, the Netherlands ranks at fifth place, up one position from the previous year.

52. The Netherlands is famously known for liberal policies as the Dutch are very accepting of individual freedoms. They accept multicultural ethnicities and Amsterdam is an example of this as it is home to nearly two hundred different ethnicities.

53. Just as you can bike around the country, you can see the country through the canals in a boat. I found out there were canal tours within all major towns I had visited. This was actually a very relaxing way to see different cities.

54. There are about 1,000 working windmills and some of these have been recognized as UNESCO World Heritage Sites.

55. The city of Amsterdam is an amazing tourist attraction that was built on poles. It is incredible to see how this city was built.

56. Dutch men are currently the tallest people in the world. Dutch women are currently the second tallest in the world, with the tallest being Latvian women. Walking amongst the crowds, I thought they all looked like giants as maybe to them, I am the tiny one.

57. Keukenhof, the world's famous tulip garden is also the world's largest flower garden. They have

wedding ceremonies there too and I hope maybe one day, I will get to see one.

58. New York City was originally called New Amsterdam and was founded as a Dutch colony.

59. The Dutch are the world's second largest agricultural exporters. It is a common phrase how the Dutch feed the world despite being almost one fourth of the size of my home state, Washington State in the United States.

60. Both Australia and New Zealand were recorded to have been first discovered by the Dutch amongst Europeans. Australia was called "New Holland" and New Zealand was named after the Dutch province of "Zeeland." As I had lived in Australia for a few years, this was a really interesting fact the tour guides had mentioned.

61. The Netherlands is one of the most densely populated countries in the European Union.

62. The Dutch are one of the world's biggest exporters of cheese and are big cheese eaters. Be sure to visit one of the amazing cheese markets in the country to have a unique experience.

63. Dutch parents have a balanced role in parenting, with many people opting for part-time jobs. I had watched

fathers pick up their children after school on family bikes. This was an amazing sight as these memories, of a father with his children on a bike, are there forever. I also watched mothers and fathers with little ones and their pets on family bikes together.

64. The Dutch are one of the largest coffee consumers in the world. On average, they drink about two to three cups per day. I drink about three cups per day. Hey, I am from Seattle, birthplace of Starbucks.

65. When renting or buying property, "unfurnished" often means without flooring, curtains, appliances, etc., so one is advised to inspect the property before renting or purchasing.

66. A common Dutch phrase is "Doe normaal!" This means, "Be normal!" This phrase is very telling of Dutch society which likes to treat everyone equally. I agree that we need to treat the whole world equally with no superiority or inferiority. This one phrase I will take with me and I believe anyone who travels to the Netherlands will pick up this phrase in a positive way.

67. Heineken is headquartered in Amsterdam, the Netherlands.

68. Once a Dutch man turns 50, he becomes "Abraham." Once a Dutch woman turns 50, she becomes, "Sarah." I had met a very nice waitress who had celebrated her fiftieth birthday and was so proud she was "Sarah" now.

69. Koningsdag (English: King's Day) is a national holiday celebrated throughout the Kingdom of the Netherlands on the ruling monarch's birthday. Koningsdag is April 27, the birthday of King Willem-Alexander.

70. The Dutch consume a lot of milk and rank third highest in the world. Many have credited their tall height to this fact.

71. It is normal for Dutch babies to be born at home as many Dutch mothers choose to give birth at home instead of at a hospital.

72. The Dutch have very high English proficiency with around 90% being able to speak English. They have the highest English proficiency outside of native English speakers in the world. If you are not a native Dutch speaker trying to speak in Dutch, they can generally tell off of your pronunciation and quickly switch to English.

73. Dutch crime is very low. Many speculate this is due to openness in areas such as prostitution, marijuana, etc. being legal. This has led to many Dutch prisons closing down.

74. Philips was founded in Eindhoven, the Netherlands and is headquartered in Amsterdam, the Netherlands.

75. The Netherlands has the least lactose intolerant people.

76. Hogeweyk is a gated village that was specifically designed for 152 seniors with dementia. This amazing village has everything a person could wish for in a village, yet this also has twenty-four-hour security and medical assistance. I believe this is amazing.

77. The largest consumers of licorice are the Dutch.

78. On the topic of equality, there is a famous phrase used internationally, "going Dutch." This refers to people having equal involvement in paying bills. It is not uncommon to split bills at a restaurant with your friend, instead of one person covering the entire bill.

79. There are 1,281 bridges in Amsterdam.

80. Warning sirens are tested publicly every month on the first Monday, unless it is a public holiday, at 12 PM. The siren lasts 1 minute and 26 seconds. If you

hear this siren multiple times, or on another day, take shelter, follow government instructions, and do what you would in times of emergency. Always be prepared as I am for I live within the foothills of Mount Rainier in Washington State. Mount Rainier is one of the most dangerous volcanoes, and we have an evacuation route in case of emergency.

81. The Dutch created the cocoa press which allowed the conversion of roasted cacao beans to cocoa powder.

82. On your birthday, you can expect to be congratulated as a birthday is compared to an achievement. This congratulations, however, is also conveyed to your children, parents, family members, or even friends.

83. The headquarters of Royal Dutch Shell is in The Hague, the Netherlands.

84. As I came to the conclusion of this book, I had to add an event the whole world just witnessed. The FIFA Women's World Cup 2019 has just taken place. My homeland the United States came first, and my dreamland the Netherlands came second. I am proud of both teams.

These are some interesting facts I have encountered through my travels and research. This is only to guide you through your travel journey. I must say, however, some of the facts change year to year. Life is a blessed journey where the sacred travelers have guided all throughout time. Through the water, air, and road, we travel to find peace and serenity. Pilgrimages are also a travel journey of the traveler who seeks peace.

The Netherlands is small European country, that has so much presence throughout this globe. All the world citizens know this country through its place upon the global stage. I knew this land through her tulip fields and her loving people who have taken a permanent place within my inner soul. I would want all of you to feel the same love I have felt by visiting this land and taking back so much more with me.

WORLD HERITAGE SITES

Mill Network at Kinderdijk-Elshout

There are many National Heritage Sites throughout the Netherlands. UNESCO has listed many historical sites around the world as World Heritage Sites including Angkor Wat of Cambodia, Taj Mahal of India, Great Barrier Reef of Australia, Giza Pyramids of Egypt, Great Wall of China, and the Yellowstone National Park of the United States. UNESCO has listed ten properties of the Kingdom of the Netherlands as World Heritage Sites. Eight of the properties are within the Netherlands, one property is in Curaçao, and one property is at the border of the Netherlands and Germany.

According to UNESCO, the following are nine cultural sites within the Netherlands and Curaçao along with the year in which each one was declared to be a World Heritage Site:

1995:   Schokland, in Noordoostpolder, in Flevoland

1996:   Defence Line of Amsterdam, in North Holland

1997:   Historic Area of Willemstad, Inner City, and Harbour, in Curaçao

1997:   Mill Network at Kinderdijk-Elshout, a village in South Holland

1999:   Droogmakerij de Beemster (Beemster Polder), north of Amsterdam, in North Holland

1998:   Ir.D.F. Woudagemaal (D.F. Wouda Steam Pumping Station) in Friesland

2000:   Rietveld Schröderhuis (Rietveld Schröder House), in Utrecht

2010:   Seventeenth-Century Canal Ring Area of Amsterdam inside the Singelgracht, in North Holland

2014:   Van Nellefabriek of Rotterdam, in South Holland

According to UNESCO, the following is one natural site within the Netherlands along with the year in which the site was declared to be a World Heritage Site:

2009, 2014:   Wadden Sea, a natural site shared between Germany and the Netherlands was declared a World Heritage Site by UNESCO in 2009. This World Heritage Site was extended to include the Danish part of the Wadden Sea in 2014.

For the travelers, whether a citizen, a tourist, or a person who wants justice at the International Court of Justice, this land is where the blessings are found. From the historical past through the present and I believe within the future too, one shall find peace in this land. You the travelers who could not make it to this land, travel forever through the pages of this book.

If life gives you a chance like life has blessed me, do travel to this land. This land cannot speak for herself, but I shall speak for this land. She sits far away from me, yet I have found my peace and serenity within this land. The children of the orange tree have spread flowers throughout this world, uniting all nations through the fields of tulips. Each tulip smiles at her grower, reminding us this is a blessing sent to you from the Netherlands.

I admire and shall always hold a special bond close to my heart with this land and the Father of the Fatherland. This is a land I was not born within, nor do I have any known bond with her. Yet I believe in the unknown and unseen love that cannot be weighed or touched, but only felt within the inner soul of the beholders.

This is a country I love and hold within my soul as a special gift given or sent to me. Love is the best gift a person can receive from anywhere. I have received this love within my inner soul for an unknown country.

Through my next chapter, I will tour this land with you, but I want you to look into a few phrases I have picked up traveling within this country. Again, her citizens are fluent in English and there was no language barrier for me as I always spoke in English. I had, however, made a lot of friends and picked up their phrases as I wanted to know their language to be able to say it in their mother tongue. The accent changes a lot as within different provinces, they have different accents or ways to say some words. I have included a few general phrases here that may make you feel included in the conversation.

COMMON PHRASES

I realized after traveling through the world, it is easier to learn a language by speaking with the locals. Embarrassment of what would they think only prevents us from learning. So go ahead and start speaking whatever you know, and your friends will help you walk through the language after that. I have promised one such Dutch friend, I will get on a bike if she can then guide me through how to stay on a bike and not fall off. Then, I will somehow stay on and move forward. Here, I have included a few Dutch phrases. Enjoy speaking Dutch.

ENGLISH	DUTCH	PRONUNCIATION
thank you	dank je wel	dahnk-yuh-vehl
you are welcome	graag gedaan	khrahkh khuh-dahn
please	alsjeblieft	ahl-shuh-bleeft
hello	hallo	hah-low
hi	hoi	hoy
bye	doei	doo-ee
I am	ik ben	ik ben
good morning	goedemorgen	khoo-duh-mawr-ghuh
good afternoon	goedemiddag	khoo-duh-mih-dahkh
good evening	goedenavond	khoo-duh-nah-fohnt
Do you speak English?	Spreek je Engels?	sprayk yuh ehng-uhls
I do not speak Dutch.	Ik spreek geen Nederlands.	ik sprayk khayn Nederlands

Oh the children of this world, come visit this sacred land. Some of you are the visiting birds who will fly back home. Some of you might hope this land adopts you within her chest. Through the pages we have gained knowledge about a country and her people. Now let us all become a tourist and tour this land in union through the next chapter I call, JOURNEY THROUGH THE TWELVE PROVINCES.

CHAPTER FOUR:

JOURNEY THROUGH THE TWELVE PROVINCES

"Come travel through the mystical land of the twelve provinces, where all her citizens and visitors find blessings from dawn through dusk through dawn."

-Ann Marie Ruby

A TRAVELER'S JOURNEY

The journey begins

Within dreams of the destination.

The capital city Amsterdam,

Hugs you within her Dam Square,

As she takes you on a walk, through history.

The traveler you are,

Trying to sit within the Parliament of a nation,

As you too can become a part of history,

Within the political capital, The Hague.

A part of the present history you become,

Now traveling to learn from the Founding Father,

Who still guides from the past as you enter the home,

Of the blue and white potteries, Delft.

With all the handicrafts,

You the traveler land upon the biggest port in Europe,

Thinking about the past, present, and future travelers,

Who landed here within Rotterdam.

The traveler you are,

Taking a journey through the land of windmills,

The land of tulips, and

The land of canals.

Carrying within your boat of memories,

You have blessings of this land.

Oh the sacred traveler,

Open your eyes and see this land through my eyes.

May this be your sacred journey,

Through the twelve provinces,

Of the Netherlands,

Through my pen and paper.

Travel within her,

As I give you the sacred key to

A TRAVELER'S JOURNEY.

A tourist I had become through my dreams as another land had called me within my dreams. Life did not give me a chance to meet the Father of the Fatherland and other citizens who had lived there as time, the enemy of life, was in between us. A father with so much love for his children, had created a land for all differences to evaporate and only blossom with beautiful colorful rainbows. At every corner, I found the real pot of gold called my love for this land.

My journey begins at dawn as my meditative mind seeks peace within my soul. Dawn breaks through as this yogini mind, body, and soul travel through all obstacles. The pilgrims have taken pilgrimages throughout time as a sacred journey for their souls. The mystics, religious gurus, archeological scientists, and even we the modern-day travelers, are all taking the same trip through time and land for our souls. Traveling unites the travelers to the land as the travelers leave behind their stories and take along memories to share with all throughout time.

I too sought the land that had come to me within my dreams. From the past through the present times, this land had crossed the door of miracles to come to this yogini. I had found her like dawn peeking through my windows. I opened the windows and found a sacred land waiting to be sought out by my soul.

In the mystical land, ancient castles stand tall with stories from the past. This land has fields of flowers that have become the romantic scenery of global movie sets. This land has canoes carrying romantic couples through canals. This land is known for the colorful tulips, windmills, canals, and famous cheese.

Come and travel within this magical land through my eyes. Let us walk through the largest cities Amsterdam, The Hague, Rotterdam, and Utrecht as we explore the provinces of North Holland, South Holland, and Utrecht first. We will then continue our journey through the provinces of Limburg,

Drenthe, Friesland, North Brabant, Zeeland, Gelderland, Flevoland, Overijssel, and Groningen.

This land has so much to offer. I have visited the land of my dreams twice, yet I could not cover all of the places I had wanted to visit. I felt even two visits were not enough to satisfy my inner soul. Some places in this world just take your heart away and you do not know why it is so. The Netherlands for me is one such country, where I have found my Heaven.

THE TWELVE PROVINCES
OF THE NETHERLANDS

Open your travel journal and take a trip with me

Through the Netherlands.

Let us travel through

The old merchant towns of North Holland, and

Through the Peace Palace within South Holland.

Oh the traveler, do journey through the past as you walk

Within the medieval buildings of Utrecht.

The traveler's journey is never complete without a dessert,

So stop over and enjoy your vlaai here in Limburg.

Get back to action and let the Wildlands Adventure Zoo

Welcome you to Drenthe.

Let us stop over and learn to speak in another language

Called Frisian within Friesland.

Oh the traveler, journey through the historic city of Breda

And see the Breda castle

As you end up within North Brabant.

Through this journal, may your dream castles be built

Upon the most beautiful beaches of Zeeland.

From the beaches, walk into the World War II

Historical past within Arnhem in Gelderland.

Sacred travelers, do stop over at the Grote Markt

And fill your eyes with the sight

Of the Martinitoren in Groningen.

Heart filled with love and joy,

May you end up within Giethoorn,

The Dutch Venice in Overijssel.

Finally the blessed travelers,

Do take back some learned lessons

From this amazing journey

As you too can see how the Dutch reclaimed their lands

Within Noordoostpolder in Flevoland.

May the pages of all sacred travelers' journals

Be completed as all but travel through

THE TWELVE PROVINCES

OF THE NETHERLANDS.

PROVINCE OF NOORD-HOLLAND

(ENGLISH: NORTH HOLLAND)

Amsterdam, the Netherlands.

AMSTERDAM

North Holland is located in the western part of the Netherlands. Amsterdam is the largest city and capital city of the Netherlands. Through her well-renowned Schiphol Airport, Amsterdam is one of the major connecting hubs between Europe and the rest of the world. I had felt at home when I had walked into one of the cafés after landing. The café had on its napkins the words "Welcome home," in both

93

English and Dutch. These napkins were a special touch that had taken a special place within my soul. The airport staff was absolutely professional and very welcoming as they told me about the train, tram, bus system, and how to travel to different places within the country.

As a frequent traveler, airport experiences can be really difficult at times and remain in the memories of a person. During these times that we have landed upon, we all need to be patient for everyone's safety. When I arrived at this airport, I felt like I had arrived home, and I absolutely miss even the airport and the staff.

Amsterdam found her name from the Amstel River and a dam that was built within the river. As a young child, I had no clue about the Netherlands, but I knew Amsterdam as one of the most popular places to visit. From a small fishing village to the famous trading center of the 17th century to the present day, Amsterdam has a rich history.

The city is completely built on poles and is known for narrow and tilting buildings. The staircases in many of the buildings are so narrow that furniture cannot be carried up. I was informed by a tour guide, they have hooks outside of many buildings to pull furniture in through the windows.

Along with Amsterdam's famous old charm, buildings, and architecture, the canals are a tourist attraction as well.

To this day, Amsterdam shares her roads with the past and the present. Ghosts of the past are known to still roam around some of the famous places of Amsterdam. The ghost of Helena is said to still roam around on Spooksteeg, the street where she lived nearly 300 years ago. Legend says Helena's sister and a sailor fell in love. Yet Helena out of jealousy murdered her sister and married the same sailor.

Helena confessed only while taking her last breath. At that time, her husband cursed her saying her spirit would always roam around. Maybe you too will see her while visiting or remember to keep a guard out if you want to see her. I believe stories like this keep the historical towns alive. While visiting, do ask your tour guides to guide you through these stories as there are so many.

It is said you can literally bike around the entire country. This is true if you know how to bike. I do not, so I had taken the canal tour through Amsterdam. For my soul, the canal tour with a tour guide and wine to sip, or nonalcoholic drinks for me such as soft drinks, was a journey of a lifetime. The following are some attractions you should consider visiting when you enter this great historical city:

1. RIJKSMUSEUM:

The Rijksmuseum was originally in The Hague. In 1808, the museum was moved to Amsterdam. This museum has the largest collection of arts within the Netherlands. Visit this museum and walk through the minds of historical painters.

2. ANNE FRANK HUIS (ANNE FRANK HOUSE):

This is the well-known house where the famous diarist Anne Frank had hidden during World War II. From this house, we have the famous writer who had taken birth even after her death. This proves even after death, life lives on through the pages of history. Enter this house and remember Anne Frank's words, "It's really a wonder that I haven't dropped all my ideals, because they seem so absurd and impossible to carry out. Yet I keep them, because in spite of everything I still believe that people are really good at heart" (263). What a blessed soul, she was and shall always be.

3. CANAL TOUR THROUGH AMSTERDAM:

The Grachtengordel (English: Canal Ring) was dug out in the early 17th century to attract the rich and famous. This attraction had taken its place within the list of UNESCO World Heritage Sites in 2010. I personally recommend all of you to take a tour through the canals, as then you will get to see Amsterdam in one day.

4. BIKE TOUR THROUGH AMSTERDAM:

The Netherlands is a country where even the King, Queen, and the Prime Minister ride bikes. You can bike through the entire city, or through the whole country. It is an amazing journey for the cyclists. I only wish I knew how to bike. I shall overcome my embarrassment of not knowing how to ride a bike, and shall learn one of these days, or maybe ride an adult tricycle.

5. AUTO RICKSHAW TOURS:

If you are familiar with auto rickshaws, you do not want to miss out on this tour in Amsterdam. I was lucky to have traveled in Delhi and Rajasthan, India by auto rickshaw while on a vacation. I absolutely love being in Europe and felt as if I was back traveling through India. Some travelers have cheese and sip wine on these tours. Those who do not bike can absolutely take this tour.

6. DAM SQUARE:

Within Dam Square, so much history is buried. One should visit this place to feel the past and the present. The future too shall unite here as time passes by us and history continues to be written here. Some of the famous witch burnings and public executions had taken place within this square. Dam Square is said to be haunted.

7. ROYAL PALACE OF AMSTERDAM:

The Royal Palace is located within Dam Square and is one of the three official palaces of the monarchs of the Netherlands.

8. VAN GOGH MUSEUM:

Vincent Willem van Gogh is an artist who is historically famous for his paintings. His life story is as famous as his paintings. One should definitely visit this museum and read about his journey through life.

9. STELLING VAN AMSTERDAM (ENGLISH: DEFENCE, OR DEFENSE, LINE OF AMSTERDAM):

The Defence Line of Amsterdam was recognized as a World Heritage Site by UNESCO in 1996. Just as the Dutch reclaimed their land from water, they also used water to protect themselves from foreign threat. The Defence Line consists of around 84 miles, or 135 kilometers of nearly 50 forts around Amsterdam. This defensive system was built from 1883 to 1920. It could be used to flood the land around Amsterdam, preventing foreign threat from entering. The water would be too shallow for boats, but deep enough so people could not come through.

10. KEUKENHOF:

Near Amsterdam, the Keukenhof is the most famous tulip garden in the world. Enjoy the romantic trip through this garden at least once in your lifetime. Even a single person like myself absolutely loves to either dream about the significant other or just enjoy Mother Earth's gifts to this world.

11. ZANDVOORT:

West of Amsterdam, Zandvoort is a seaside resort by the North Sea. If possible, check out an event at the nearby racetrack, Circuit Zandvoort.

12. DROOGMAKERIJ DE BEEMSTER (ENGLISH: BEEMSTER POLDER):

This project was undertaken in the early 17th century as advanced technology allowed the Dutch to reclaim land and create this exceptional polder. The Beemster Polder was named after the Beemster Lake which was drained in 1612 to reclaim this land. It was such an amazing project and was named by UNESCO as a World Heritage Site in 1999. Within the Beemster Polder are many villages, and forts that are part of the Defence Line of Amsterdam. As you visit Amsterdam, this is a project one should visit. Take the lessons with you to other low-lying countries where you can use this technology to reclaim land and save lives from devastating floods.

Although I had stayed in The Hague, traveling to Amsterdam was very easy. Even if you do not use a car or bike, Amsterdam is connected to the whole country through train, tram, bus, or ferry system.

Zaanse Schans, the Netherlands.

ZAANSE SCHANS

A small Dutch town near Amsterdam has within her air, the smell of fresh baked breads as the famous windmills spread this aroma throughout the air. This town is a tourist attraction for the Dutch and the international visitors. You can go on a day trip to Zaanse Schans. Historic windmills and green wooden houses were brought here to recreate the look of 18th and 19th century windmills and houses. Bring the whole family as here you can also see wooden clog carvings, barrel making, and other handicrafts.

See the windmills and beautiful houses which dreams are made out of. Maybe you can convert your dreams into reality within this town. I would love to live in this kind of a village where romantic stories are made.

Haarlem, the Netherlands.

HAARLEM

With cobblestone roads, gabled houses, and tulip fields all around, is a romantic city known to all as the capital of North Holland, Haarlem. Her close proximity to Amsterdam makes for an easy day trip for the travelers. This is a place set up for the romantic pictures of a lifetime. The canals within this country give a traveler his or her complete tour of the city with peace. You can go and tour this city through the canals and find out for yourself how romantic this city is. Some sites to visit in Haarlem are as follows:

103

1. GROTE HOUTSTRAAT:

Walk through the streets and go on a shopping tour through this city as many of the Dutch call this the best shopping street. Grote Houtstraat is the longest shopping street in Haarlem.

2. HOFJES:

Hofjes were made by rich citizens for poor women who were single or widowed. Haarlem is a city known for hofjes. The hofjes are basically small houses which overlook into courtyards. Hofje van Bakenes is the oldest existing known hofje that dates back to 1395. Here, you can find single and widowed women living out the rest of their lives.

3. GROTE MARKT:

This is one of the biggest marketplaces where you can find cheese, spices, used and new clothing, and much more. This market is always lively as it always has a festival happening within the square. Another attraction within this square is the Grote Kerk.

4. GROTE KERK:

This historic church was built in the 13th century. Originally a Catholic cathedral, now it is a Protestant Church. This church was struck by lightning and parts of it had burned down. This church had gone down the lanes of obstacles, but now stands tall as an example of triumph. Do visit this church and be a part of history as you can feel the past watching over the present.

5. MOLEN DE ADRIAAN (ENGLISH: DE ADRIAAN WINDMILL):

The famous windmill of Haarlem is a stopover for all hearts. For me personally, windmills are reminders of love stories being brewed within the air. This windmill was originally built in 1778. De Adriaan caught on fire in 1932, but was brought back to life and restored again in 2002.

This windmill stands tall on the Spaarne River, watching over all the passengers passing by in the canal. Sit and enjoy an amazing sight of Dutch heritage. For me, the Netherlands and all the sacred windmills are blessings for my eyes.

PROVINCE OF ZUID-HOLLAND

(ENGLISH: SOUTH HOLLAND)

Peace Palace in The Hague, the Netherlands.

THE HAGUE

South Holland is in the western part of the Netherlands. The third largest city in the Netherlands after Amsterdam and Rotterdam is The Hague. The Hague is the capital of South Holland. While The Hague is not the capital of the Netherlands, the city is the political seat of the country from where the government rules. The King, Queen, and

Prime Minister all live and work in The Hague. The Hague is also my favorite place on Earth because of the historical buildings and rich history.

During World War II, many buildings and cities in the Netherlands were damaged by German troops. Many of the buildings in The Hague, however, retained their original architecture due to Dutch resilience. In the Battle for The Hague, the Germans had planned to take control over The Hague and capture former Queen Wilhelmina as well as Dutch politicians. Germany had planned that this invasion would cause the Netherlands to surrender to Germany.

While lives were lost, and buildings were damaged, the German plan to take over The Hague ultimately failed because of the Dutch troops' counterefforts. After the Germans horrifically bombed Rotterdam, also historically known as the Rotterdam Blitz, the Netherlands was forced to surrender. Toward the end of World War II, the Netherlands was liberated on May 5, 1944.

The Dutch have since then, rebuilt The Hague which still has much of the original historical and gothic look. Original historical buildings and castles remain to this day, present with all the memories of the past. The land, the buildings, and the trees all remain, keeping memories alive. All that have changed are the faces of us the humans.

The Hague is a romantic city or a political backdrop for the politicians. I always say, perception is but the personal perspective of the personal mind. For many, this is where the politicians sit and rule. I walked within this city and found beautiful buildings. There were old churches, palaces where the kings and queens had lived, museums, paintings, and historical houses. In the middle of Het Plein, near the Binnenhof where the Dutch Government sits, is a statue of the Founding Father watching over his nation, the visitors, Dutch leaders, and The Hague skyline.

Yes, a political backdrop of the Netherlands you might call her. Yet I found her very romantic. The serenity of this world evolves within her. Peace and serenity blanket this city from within herself. I had taken a day trip through the canals of The Hague. The architecture of The Hague was like watching a portrait within a museum. All the buildings looked like they were created with the hands of a talented painter. Yet these buildings were very much standing in front of me. Viewing these buildings, I thought how these buildings had united this traveler to the past lives of this city through our travel journeys.

You too would be lost within the history of the past. You will see each of the historic buildings has its own story to share with all the time travelers. One of the historical stories that I heard during the canal tour through The Hague was about a blacksmith's house. The blacksmith had wanted all to know this was his house and had named the house in his wife's name. I also saw the school where the Prime Minister of the Netherlands, Mark Rutte, still teaches to this day. Even after becoming the Prime Minister, he still goes to teach as this gives him peace and serenity.

We went by a restaurant on the side of the canal, where they lower a basket with food for you when you order from your boat. The tour guide pointed out historical homes with fake windows because if there were bigger, real windows, the tax rate would have gone up. Some of these buildings also had fake roof lines to make the houses look bigger.

Another story shared by our tour guide that also stayed with me as we went down the canals of The Hague, is there were some houses where widows were placed when their husbands had passed away. These were spaces for women to basically stay for the time they had left to live. Well, I guess this could be taken any way you want. In one way, at least they had a roof over their heads. Yet in another way, what was of their lives and how did these women feel living like this and waiting for what? Only history knows as these personal stories remain just that, personal within the walls of the houses.

The Hague is where history is alive within the walls of the buildings. I feel history talks to us from these walls. The Hague is a city that brings the past and present into one home through the historical buildings, art, and museums. This city shares her border with the North Sea as she flows by carrying the memories from the past to the present, taking them to the future.

The Hague is an international city with cuisines from all across the globe. One of the favorites here is Indonesian food as Indonesia was a Dutch colony. The Indonesian food is known to be a favorite of the current Prime Minister. Do visit The Hague, the Netherlands, if you are ever in Europe. If I could choose just one place to visit in the Netherlands, my choice would be The Hague. Some places to visit in The Hague are as follows:

1. BINNENHOF COMPLEX:

Binnenhof (English: inner court), a thirteenth century Gothic castle, was converted to be the political center of the Dutch in 1584. This is the oldest House of Parliament in the world which is still in use. It is in the city center of The Hague, the Netherlands. The city accommodates the Ministry of General Affairs, the office of the Prime Minister, and the States General of the Netherlands. As this is a Gothic castle, remember to keep all the lanterns of hope glowing as you walk through this complex. A tour guide had recommended visiting Binnenhof at night to see the majestic Gothic beauty.

2. VREDESPALEIS (ENGLISH: PEACE PALACE):

On August 28, 1913, the Peace Palace was born. Andrew Carnegie funded the Peace Palace knowing "The Hague was no ordinary location. As Carnegie knew very well, the city was strongly linked to the history of international law." (Gregorian 2). The International Court of Justice is located within the Peace Palace.

Andrew Dickson White's dreams were the main instrumental inspiration behind this place.

"In the words of American diplomat Andrew Dickson White, the friend who helped convince Carnegie to invest in the initial venture, the Peace Palace would serve as a 'temple of peace where the doors are open, in contrast to the Janus-temple, in times of peace and closed in cases of war.' Finally, after many long centuries, a court 'has thrown open its doors for the peaceful settlement of differences between peoples'" (Gregorian 3).

From all over the world, people come to find justice here. If ever in The Hague, then do stop over and take a tour of the Peace Palace. You can also take an audio tour at the Visitor's Center. When visiting, do not forget to tie a ribbon on the wishing tree. I had tied one there myself.

3. MAURITSHUIS (ENGLISH: MAURICE HOUSE):

Mauritshuis is an amazing art museum in The Hague, the Netherlands. This building is next to where the Prime Minister works. John Maurice, Prince of Nassau-Siegen had bought land near

Binnenhof in 1631. Later on that plot, Mauritshuis was built as a home and now is government property.

This museum is home to the Royal Cabinet of Paintings, mostly from the Dutch Golden Age. Some famous names include Johannes Vermeer, Rembrandt Harmenszoon van Rijn, and more. This building is also listed within the top 100 Dutch Heritage Sites.

When visiting the Binnenhof, one must take a stop at this museum. Then, you can make a stop at my favorite place to eat in The Hague. My favorite snack is the vegetarian bitterballen with cheese and jalapeños, which I had in Het Plein.

4. PALEIS NOORDEINDE (ENGLISH: NOORDEINDE PALACE):

Noordeinde Palace is one of the three official palaces of the Dutch Royal family and is used as the working palace for King Willem-Alexander. If the flag is up, the King is in the palace. You might be lucky enough to see the King and Queen, or even the Prime Minister on his bike while visiting this palace.

5. MADURODAM:

Madurodam is an amusement park. Complete replica models of significant Dutch buildings and architecture are made in a scale of 1:25 in Madurodam. Proceeds from this park go to different charities throughout the Netherlands.

This park was created by a mother and father to honor their son who had fought for his country. George Maduro had fought the Nazi Occupation, was captured, and died in the Dachau Concentration Camp in 1945. In 1946, this son of the Netherlands was awarded "Military Order of William," the highest and oldest decoration within the Kingdom of the Netherlands. I absolutely loved walking through this park as I could see the love of a mother and father, felt throughout time.

6. MUSEUM DE GEVANGENPOORT (ENGLISH: PRISON GATE MUSEUM):

The Gevangenpoort is located on the Buitenhof. Originally, it was the gate for the Binnenhof complex used by the Counts of Holland. Later, this was the entrance into the Buitenhof. The

Gevangenpoort is famous for being used as a prison for dangerous criminals in the medieval eras.

One prisoner was Cornelis de Witt, brother of Johan de Witt. Cornelis de Witt was accused of conspiring against William III of Orange. When Johan de Witt had gone to visit his brother in the Gevangenpoort, both brothers were murdered gruesomely. The Gevangenpoort is now a museum open to the public as visitors can walk through history and gruesome stories of torture and murder.

It is advised, however, not to take young children or those weak at heart, because of the horrific weapons and stories shown. The Buitenhof is also listed in the top 100 Dutch Heritage Sites and today has a statue of Johan de Witt.

7. SCHEVENINGEN:

Scheveningen is a seaside resort overlooking the North Sea in The Hague. Scheveningen houses the Scheveningen Lighthouse, Ferris wheel, pier, Grand Hotel Amrâth Kurhaus, and much more. The original famous bathhouse in Scheveningen was built in 1818 by Jacobus Pronk as a small wooden house with a saltwater tub. Ten years later, the bathhouse was replaced by the municipal bathhouse Grand Hôtel des Bains. This had finally been turned into the Grand Hotel Amrâth Kurhaus. As you visit Scheveningen, do walk into the Grand Hotel Amrâth Kurhaus and remember its rich history. Maybe you will feel the aura of the past travelers within this great hotel. From all around Europe, people would come here to the bathhouse to rest and recuperate with the healing sea water.

During World War II, many Dutch people determined who were German spies based on their pronunciation of the word Scheveningen. Walk within this beach and feel the blessings of the past, present, and future, as you see all is but alive through the blessed sea as she is a witness to all throughout time.

8. HUIS TEN BOSCH:

Huis Ten Bosch is the current official residence of the Dutch Royal Family. What I loved about this is that the Royal Family chose to live amongst the citizens and not away, as they live in the city center of The Hague. For royal history lovers, you definitely do not want to miss this palace.

9. JAPANESE GARDEN IN CLINGENDAEL PARK:

The Japanese Garden is only open for eight weeks annually. If you are lucky enough to be visiting when the park is open, definitely do not miss the Japanese Garden. Marguerite M. Baroness van Brienen, or Lady Daisy, then owner of the Clingendael Estate, traveled extensively to Japan. She brought various garden aspects from Japan to the Netherlands, creating what is now the only Japanese Garden in the Netherlands from the early 20th century.

10. DE PASSAGE (ENGLISH: THE PASSAGE):

Covered shopping streets were once very popular in the 1800s. Now, however, only one covered shopping street remains in the Netherlands, the Passage. I actually spent a lot of time walking through the Passage. I found most of my souvenirs and gifts to bring back home at the Passage.

Here, I have listed a few of my favorite places to visit within The Hague. If I could, I would spend my whole life here and still not have enough of this amazing city. Now let us travel to another place I also had a spiritual meditative awakening within. You know her as Delft, the Netherlands.

New Church in Delft, the Netherlands.

DELFT

Delft is located between The Hague and Rotterdam. I wanted to visit this city for all of her historical figures. The Nieuwe Kerk (English: New Church), the Oude Kerk (English: Old Church), and the Museum Prinsenhof of Delft, have still to this day the past inhabitants living through the memories of life.

From the Old Church, I had walked to the New Church where the Dutch Founding Father, William the Silent, had been laid to rest. Delft reminded me of an old romantic movie set, with beautiful historical buildings still standing tall with history buried within them. Walk through this town where you will find yourself admiring the canals, boat tours, old antique shopping centers, and enjoy your walk through history. Some places to visit when in Delft are as follows:

1. NIEUWE KERK (ENGLISH: NEW CHURCH):

The New Church in Delft has a private Royal Family crypt to accommodate the coffins of the Dutch Royal Family. The Founding Father of the Netherlands, William the Silent was interred there in 1584. The entrance leading to the crypt is blocked off with a very heavy stone. Only the Dutch Royal Family members are allowed to go down into the Royal Family crypt.

Within the New Church, however, you can view a miniature replica of the crypt inside a display case. Visitors can also see the grand mausoleum made for William the Silent. You can climb the 376 steps of the New Church. The tower itself is around 357 feet, or 108.75 meters in height. One of my friends climbed to the top of the tower and came back to our group inside the New Church, all while we were still talking with the tour guide, which must have been quite long.

2. OUDE KERK (ENGLISH: OLD CHURCH):

The Old Church in Delft is an amazing structure. It is famous as its tower with a height of around 246 feet, or 75 meters, actually leans and tilts over slightly. The leaning church tower is taller than the Leaning Tower of Pisa. Within this Gothic Protestant Church, there are numerous memorial stones and mausoleums for historical figures even to this day. Do visit this site as it is within walking distance to the New Church.

3. MUSEUM PRINSENHOF:

Museum Prinsenhof is the house of William the Silent where he was murdered on July 10, 1584. This historical site to this day is a witness to that horrific event. On the wall, near the staircase, you can still see the holes from the bullets that had taken William the Silent's life.

In 1572, William the Silent had moved into the Convent of St Agatha and converted it to his home. The nuns were allowed to live out their stay, yet new nuns were not permitted afterward as this was then known as the Prinsenhof. You can visit the old chapel room and multiple levels exhibiting the history of the Netherlands, the life of William the Silent, and the history of Delft.

4. SINT AGATHAPLEIN:

Sint Agathaplein (English: Saint Agatha Square), is a small square in front of the Prinsenhof. There is a small garden with the statue of William the Silent and boxwood hedges planted all around it. This was a place where the nuns had resided until they were not allowed to live there anymore. I would recommend all of you to go and sit at Sint Agathaplein and meditate as you enjoy your drink or food. This was an amazing place for my soul. My friends and I ordered latte macchiatos which we enjoyed at Sint Agathaplein.

5. DELFT POTTERY:

The Dutch famous blue and white pottery factory may be toured north of Delft. Once you have made your way through the Netherlands, you must go home with some famous blue and white pottery from Delft. Two famous factories known to still create these potteries are Royal Delft and De Delftse Pauw, in Rijswijk, the Netherlands.

6. CANAL TOURS:

To enjoy the historical city of Delft completely, one must take a trip through the canals. On this trip, you get to sit and sail through history with William the Silent and all historical figures yet within the present time. There are a lot of companies providing boat tours through the canals and yes you might even see a wedding couple taking a tour through the same canal too.

Delft is a town filled with history and the historical figures walk with you through the memories of the tour guides. I had an amazing walk through the town center where I had spent a day, yet I feel like I could have spent a lifetime and not get bored. Life around Delft is very lively with the leaning tower of the Old Church sitting in the middle, reminding all of us about the historical figures of the past.

As I was about to leave Delft, I had dined at a place behind the City Hall called De Waag. This restaurant was originally a weighing house, where goods were weighed and just maybe witches. De Waag is now a restaurant and an amazing building just to be in. As I left Delft and later went toward Rotterdam, I had the New Church and its inhabitants within my prayers throughout my stay within the Netherlands and even to this day.

Rotterdam, the Netherlands.

ROTTERDAM

Rotterdam is the second largest city in the Netherlands with the biggest port in Europe. A dam was created near the Rotte River, a river in the Rhine-Meuse-Scheldt delta, after people had come and settled there in the 13th century. Rotterdam, however, was almost completely destroyed during World War II. After the war, the city was completely rebuilt from the ground up.

This is the reason even today Rotterdam is architecturally very different from other Dutch cities. Rotterdam, however, always gets lost within the shadows of Amsterdam, as people compare the two. I personally believe the two cities are very different with their own individual identities.

I had traveled to Rotterdam from The Hague by train and it was an easy commute. I enjoyed the scenic ride. The Dutch citizens are very friendly and helpful as English is widely spoken by all. Now through my eyes, let us travel through this great city:

1. EUROMAST:

In 1960, Architect H. A. Maaskant had designed this observation tower in Rotterdam to showcase an indoor flower show. Originally, the tower was around 328 feet, or 100 meters tall. In 1970, the space tower was added which made the structure around 607 feet, or 185 meters tall. This is not the tallest building in the Netherlands, but this is the highest watch tower. The views from this tower are spectacular on clear days as you have a 360 degree view of Rotterdam. The revolving lift takes you to the observation tower. When visiting, you should definitely watch the sunset. There is a restaurant there where you can order breakfast, lunch, or dinner. You may be able to see Antwerp, a city within Belgium.

2. GROTE OF SINT-LAURENSKERK:

The all stone basilica was built between 1449 and 1525. In 1572, this church was a Protestant Church. On May 14, 1940, World War II had left this building heavily damaged. Yet this is the only medieval structure still standing after World War II in Rotterdam. This building was only restored, not rebuilt.

The building is amazing as it had attracted my attention without any tour guide. I had spent a day in the open farmers' market. I walked into this church as I was mesmerized by the architecture which dominated through its presence within the modern buildings. I had lit a candle and prayed within the church.

The building has a huge organ in the middle giving the feeling of peace and serenity. There are some alcoves with ancient gravesites. You can take an audio tour as you walk through this amazing church.

3. EUROPOORT:

Situated by the Rhine and the Meuse, Europoort is one of the world's busiest ports. As the connection between Rotterdam and the North Sea was poor, the canal Nieuwe Waterweg (English: New Waterway) was created to connect the Rhine and the Meuse to the North Sea. This canal was deepened several times throughout the years and gave birth to the largest port in Europe. This port is called the Gate to Europe.

4. CUBE HOUSE:

Architect Piet Blom had designed these 1,100 square feet, or 100 square meter, cubic houses above pedestrian bridges. Blom had wanted them to look like a sea of trees. These houses stand out as an amazing site to the tourists. You might feel claustrophobic living within these houses as the windows and walls are angled at 54.7 degrees. It also might be an adventure of a lifetime living in these houses. Personally, I would love to take pictures of these houses as I might feel dizzy living in them. These pictures are definitely worth being kept within your travel journals.

5. WITTE HUIS (ENGLISH: WHITE HOUSE):

In 1898, the first hoogbouw (English: high rise building) to be built in Europe was the Witte Huis. This is a National Heritage Site in Rotterdam. The building was designed by William Molenbroek. The Witte Huis is also one of the few buildings that survived World War II. The old and new blend in here so well, it is definitely not what one would expect.

6. MARKTHAL (ENGLISH: MARKET HALL):

Queen Máxima had opened the Market Hall on October 1, 2014. This horseshoe shaped unique marketplace was designed by the architectural firm MVRDV of Rotterdam. This complex also has apartments, retail stores, and underground parking.

The Market Hall stands out for its unique design and one should stop over here when visiting Rotterdam.

7. VAN NELLEFABRIEK (ENGLISH: VAN NELLE FACTORY):

Situated in Rotterdam, this industrial factory was built in the 1920s. The concept was taken from North American and European designs. The factory was used to produce coffee, tea, and tobacco. Today, the factory holds different businesses. This factory is very different from what you would think a factory looks like. The steel and glass façade is modern and allows a lot of natural light to enter. The Van Nelle Factory made an amazing use of space and took its place amongst the UNESCO World Heritage Sites in 2014.

8. MOLENS VAN KINDERDIJK-ELSHOUT (ENGLISH: MILL NETWORK AT KINDERDIJK-ELSHOUT):

Step into the past as you take a 30-minute waterbus ride from Rotterdam to the village of 19 windmills from the 1700s. These windmills are no longer in use but stand as evidence of how the Dutch used hydraulic engineering to protect their land from flooding. This historical village of windmills was listed as a World Heritage Site by UNESCO in 1997.

9. ROTTERDAM HARBOR:

Before ending the Rotterdam tour, one must go and take a harbor tour through Europe's largest port. As you cruise through the harbor on your water taxi, boat, or any kind of water vessel, remember to sit and enjoy this ride. I would recommend doing this last as then you can go back through your memory lane and revisit your personal tour of the city, through the water.

The tall skyscrapers are all within your view as you sail through the harbor with peace and serenity. History also guides you through the memory lanes of the past as your tour guides retell history through the recollection of memories.

PROVINCE OF UTRECHT

Dom Tower and Jan van Nassau monument in Utrecht, the Netherlands.

UTRECHT

Utrecht is in the middle of the Netherlands. The capital of the province is the fourth largest city in the

Netherlands and has the same name, Utrecht. The city is recognized as the religious center of the Netherlands. Nearby within the province of Utrecht, is the birthplace of King Willem-Alexander. His mother, former Queen and now Princess Beatrix of the Netherlands, currently resides in her Drakensteyn Castle. Her son Prince Friso of Orange-Nassau is buried near her castle which was his childhood home.

1. DOM TOWER:

The amazing church tower is visible throughout the city and has been the icon of the Utrecht skyline for hundreds of years since it was built in 1382. This is the tallest building in Utrecht and is the highest church tower within the Netherlands. You can also climb the 465 steps of the DOM tower and see this city from high above.

2. DOMUNDER:

Take your flashlights and enter the underground journey through the Roman ruins in DOMunder. This is an entrance to an underground space where you can view two thousand years of Dutch history.

3. HET SPOORWEGMUSEUM (ENGLISH: THE RAILWAY MUSEUM):

For a family adventure, make sure no one misses out on this one. This museum is located in the former Station Utrecht Maliebaan. The Railway Museum has a large selection of antique historic trains. The 175-year-old Dutch train history has been recreated and is alive within this museum. While visiting, you would wonder if you have actually traveled time.

4. KASTEEL DE HAAR (ENGLISH: DE HAAR CASTLE):

Just outside of the city of Utrecht, within the province of Utrecht, sits the largest castle of the Netherlands. I had taken a tour through this castle and felt like I had lived within the past, where there were moats, suspension bridges, towers, and much more. Next to the castle, there was a romantic chapel. I had seen a couple was preparing to get married while I waited for my coffee at the café. Do take a tour through the beautiful gardens and the castle when you visit Utrecht.

5. PYRAMID OF AUSTERLITZ:

This national monument stands at around 118 feet, or 36 meters tall in Woudenberg, the Netherlands. The Pyramid of Austerlitz was originally built in 1804 by French General Auguste de Marmont and his army, as he was inspired by the Great Pyramid of Giza. There is a stone obelisk on top of this pyramid which was built in 1894 as the original wooden one had deteriorated over time.

The complete pyramid had been restored quite a few times as it had deteriorated. The pyramid was finally re-opened to the public in 2008, after years of restoration. When in Utrecht, do stop over and visit this pyramid.

6. RIETVELD SCHRÖDERHUIS (ENGLISH: RIETVELD SCHRÖDER HOUSE):

This was an amazing private residence, now a museum, designed in 1924 by architect Gerrit Thomas Rietveld for homeowner Truus Schröder-Schräder. The architectural design followed De Stijl (English: The Style), a Dutch art movement. UNESCO listed the house as a World Heritage Site in 2000.

7. HEKSENWAAG (ENGLISH: WITCHES' WEIGHHOUSE OR MUSEUM DE WAAG):

From throughout Europe, from the mid-15th century through the 18th century, witches were being burned at stake. As hope became bleak, innocent men and women tried to find hope even within a faraway land. One such place where they found hope is known as Oudewater. The Holy Roman Emperor Charles V had ordered for those accused of being a witch to be weighed. If they weigh nothing, then they would be burned, but as humans weigh something, they would be set free.

This place is famous for setting these hopeful hearts free as they came to prove to the world, they too were human but accused for various reasons. Some accusations were even linked simply to jealousy. Do visit this place as it still holds the memories of so many who were set free. Freedom is something we live for as our birthright. Yet these people had to fight for their freedom. Today, without fear, you can visit this place, and be weighed on the original scales. No one will accuse you of being a witch.

PROVINCE OF LIMBURG

Maastricht, the Netherlands.

Limburg is located within the southeastern part of the Netherlands. The capital city is Maastricht. This province borders Germany and Belgium. The highest point within the Netherlands, the Vaalserberg (English: Vaals mountain) is located within this province. The Vaalserberg is around 1,058 feet, or 322 meters tall.

Maastricht is one of the oldest cities in the Netherlands, which the tourist should visit. In this old city, there are 1,677 National Heritage Sites. The 1992 Maastricht

Treaty was signed in this city, bringing forth the European Union and the euro. The city is full of rich history. You may even stroll underground through tunnels and caves with a guide, exploring where people had hidden during World War II.

Limburg is also famous for the Roermond Witch Trials. These trials had taken place between 1613 and 1616. On the Galgenberg hill in the Kapel in 't Zand (English: Chapel in 't Zand), at least 64 people were burned to death at the stake, after being accused of witchcraft.

PROVINCE OF DRENTHE

Hunebedden in the province of Drenthe, the Netherlands.

The province of Drenthe is located within the northeastern part of the country. The capital city is Assen. Anyone interested in cycling or history should visit this province. Drenthe is very popular for cycling. Drenthe is also known as the cycling paradise of the Netherlands. Drenthe has more than 1,300 miles, or 2,100 kilometers of cycling paths. The Union Cycliste Internationale, a sports association that governs cycling globally, honored the province in 2016 with the UCI Bike Region label not only for holding cycling events but also for initiatives taken to advance cycling within the province ("Cycling for All").

Historic Drenthe has artifacts dating back 150,000 years which were found here from the Wolstonian stage. Hunebedden (English: dolmens) are single chamber prehistoric tombs. These are the oldest monuments in the city of Borger. These tombs are from 3,000 to 3,500 BC. There are 54 of these tombs that are still standing. The stone used are believed to have been left from the Ice Age.

The Netherlands is a flat country and the type of stones that were used are typically found in Scandinavia. The stones may have arrived in the Netherlands during the Ice Age. Near the stones were found different artifacts related to the same era. How all of these heavy stones came is still a mystery linked within the hidden doors of the past.

Today there is a museum called Hunebed Centre where one can travel time and see how previous civilizations are believed to have looked like and how they lived. These Hunebedden are believed to have been built before the Pyramids of Egypt and the Stonehenge. Some even say these burial chambers must have been built by giants. When traveling to the Netherlands for a vacation, I suggest taking a tour through this prehistoric time.

PROVINCE OF FRYSLÂN

(ENGLISH: FRIESLAND)

The Oldehove in Leeuwarden, the Netherlands.

The official languages in Friesland are Frisian and Dutch. In this province, you will see the Oldehove tower within the capital Leeuwarden. The tower was being built between 1529 and 1533. The tower was never completed, yet the tower remains standing with a height of nearly 128 feet, or 39 meters. The tower stands tall, tilting over the city.

Also within Friesland is the D.F. Wouda Steam Pumping Station which is the largest steam powered pumping station. This pumping station was opened in the town of Lemmer by former Queen Wilhelmina on October 7, 1920. The D.F. Wouda Steam Pumping Station continues to protect the province from floods and is listed as a World Heritage Site by UNESCO since 1998.

PROVINCE OF NOORD-BRABANT

(ENGLISH: NORTH BRABANT)

Monument of painter Hieronymus Bosch in 's-Hertogenbosch,
the Netherlands.

North Brabant is located within the southern part of Netherlands. The capital city is 's-Hertogenbosch, also known as Den Bosch. The famous painter Hieronymus Bosch was from this town. Within the Market Square, there is a statue of the famous painter. This province is famous for Bossche bol pastries, fortresses, and medieval characteristics. Do pick up the pastries once you are here. This province also had given birth to the famous painter, Vincent Willem van Gogh. You can still visit his home in Zundert.

Eindhoven is also a city the tourist should visit, as this is the design capital of the Netherlands and has the country's second largest airport. Stratumseind is the longest nightlife street within the Benelux (Belgium, Netherlands, and Luxembourg). The street is around 738 feet, or 225 meters long, with about 25,000 visitors per week. Philips, an electronic giant, was founded in 1891 by Gerard Philips and his father within Eindhoven. The headquarters of Philips is in Amsterdam.

PROVINCE OF ZEELAND

Delta Works in Zeeland, the Netherlands.

Zeeland is within the southwestern part of the Netherlands. The capital city is Middelburg. The Scheldt, the Rhine, and the Meuse rivers, come and meet within this land. A land where the three rivers meet is also known as a river delta.

The world-famous Delta Works is located within Zeeland. The nearly five miles, or eight kilometers long, the Oosterscheldekering (English: Eastern Scheldt Storm Surge Barrier) can be closed off within 75 minutes to prevent a destructive flood from ever damaging the land or her people again. Another part of the Delta Works is known as the Maeslantkering (English: Maeslant Storm Surge Barrier) which is located within Hoek van Holland (English: Hook of Holland).

This barrier has large floating structures which when needed can be filled with water, causing them to sink and become solid flood barriers. This is something I believe the world should visit and take back home the learned lessons to save life, livestock, and land. For my personal soul, I would absolutely love to sit within the mouth of the delta where all three rivers have united. Do stop by and visit Breskens, a harbor town which is also the home to the oldest cast iron lighthouse.

PROVINCE OF GELDERLAND

John Frost Bridge over the Rhine River in Arnhem, the Netherlands.

Located within the eastern part of the Netherlands, bordering Germany, Gelderland is the largest province in the Netherlands. Gelderland is home to various castles and manor houses. The travelers should stop over as they are traveling through this province. The capital of this province is Arnhem.

Arnhem is one of the cities within Liberation Route Europe, which is a route connecting eight countries that resisted the Nazis during World War II. Arnhem is known for the Battle of Arnhem during World War II. The city was heavily damaged during the war, but she remembers the victims who had tried to liberate the country. Touring through this place, you should try to visit the Airborne Museum Hartenstein where you can see exhibitions and experience the battles of World War II.

PROVINCE OF GRONINGEN

Martinitoren in Groningen, the Netherlands.

Groningen is located within the most northeastern part of the Netherlands. Here you would end up on the most famous walking trail, known as the Pieterpad (English: Pieter Path). This trail starts at the most northeastern part of the country in the village of Pieterburen and ends just south of Maastricht in the province of Limburg. The trail basically covers the whole eastern side of the Netherlands.

The capital of the province of Groningen has the same name, Groningen. This is a university city, also famous for the Martinitoren (English: Martini Tower). The Martinitoren was built 500 years ago. The city was built around the tower, as the tower's height protected the city from foreign enemies. Do not miss the bells of Martinitoren as these bells are famous throughout Europe. Remember to visit the adjacent Martinikerk (English: Martini Church), which is the oldest church in Groningen. For the lovers of old architecture, this church was originally built in the 13th century, and rebuilt and repaired later.

Do visit the Vesting Bourtange (English: Fort Bourtange), which dates back to 1580. Bourtange is a fortress town that is star-shaped with canals and dikes near the border of Germany. This famous town also has reenactments of the famous Eighty Years' War.

PROVINCE OF OVERIJSSEL

Giethoorn, the Netherlands.

Overijssel is located within the eastern part of the Netherlands, and borders Germany to one side. The capital city is Zwolle. Within this province you can find the village of Giethoorn, which has many nicknames such as the Venice of the North and the Dutch Venice. One must travel here by boat, bike, or foot. Peace and serenity are blessed to have made a home here as there are no vehicles going through this village. Giethoorn has over 180 bridges to walk around. Known as a tourist's haven, I believe this is a romantic place to be within.

150

PROVINCE OF FLEVOLAND

Old port in Schokland, the Netherlands.

Flevoland is located within the center of the country. The capital city is Lelystad. Flevoland was the last province of the Netherlands to come into existence after land was reclaimed from the Zuiderzee. Within the capital city, there are numerous museums including the Batavialand museum that goes over 7,000 years of Dutch history.

Schokland was once an island in the Zuiderzee, but constantly experienced flooding, and had land being taken under water. When land was reclaimed forming Flevoland,

151

this historic island of Schokland also rose above water as a part of the Noordoostpolder. With so much history and artifacts rising with the land, UNESCO declared Schokland as the first UNESCO World Heritage Site in the Netherlands in 1995. Do visit the Schokland Museum to learn more about the land's history.

Do you ever wonder about lighthouse keepers who had guided ships throughout time? In Schokland, when residents were evacuated, only a few stayed back including the lighthouse keeper. To this day, you can go and visit the former home of the lighthouse keeper and the ruins of the former lighthouse.

Within this journey of life, try to come and visit the land of peace and serenity, where even the Peace Palace has found her home. May we the travelers who stay here for a day, or a lifetime find the same peace all have but sought and found. Now travel through the next chapter to find out why I love this country as I call the next chapter, WHY I LOVE THE NETHERLANDS.

CONCLUSION CHAPTER:

WHY I LOVE THE NETHERLANDS

"Dreams are gifts from Heavens above, yet they must be accomplished through the life of a traveler for then dreams become reality as the diary is complete."

-Ann Marie Ruby

HEAVEN ON EARTH

Standing by the shores of the North Sea, I found you.

Within the land of tulips, I welcomed you.

Like the wind beneath the colorful windmills, I felt you.

For you are peace.

You are serenity.

You are my freedom.

For as I found you,

I found myself.

For you, I have awakened.

Your water, land, air, sun, and space healed my inner soul.

The traveler I had become, searching for peace.

Finally, peace found me.

Peace came and blessed my soul,

As I finally found within,

The Kingdom of the Netherlands,

My blessed,

HEAVEN ON EARTH.

Dreams are where the doors of the unknown had opened up and allowed me to enter a magical land called the Netherlands. I believe in dreams as my sacred dreams have guided me throughout my life. Dreams have today shown me that they have meanings as they come from Heavens above.

Carl Jung had said, "Dreams are the guiding words of the soul. Why should I henceforth not love my dreams and not make their riddling images into objects of my daily consideration?" (132). I understand what this great man whom I admire wanted to say. Dreams are guidance from the beyond we must pay attention to. For this reason, I too have flown into the land that calls me to visit her.

I have written extensively about my personal dreams within my books, *Eternal Truth: The Tunnel Of Light* and *Spiritual Lighthouse: The Dream Diaries Of Ann Marie Ruby*. I walk with my personal belief in dreams as guidance from above, supported by my research of scientific, religious, and mystical scholars. My dreams have brought me to a country that was unknown to me, yet I knew so much about her within my dreams. As I walked through the land, I felt I had revisited my dreams.

I know this land and I have a blessed connection through my love for this land, her citizens, and all of her history. I was pulled to her through the union bridge of love. I do not know the reasoning, but I believe the land wanted me to talk about her as I see her. I believe the Founding Father also wants this Earth to unite all nations, cultures, and religions for the sake of humanity. To find peace within your soul, travel to wherever you find peace. This could be within your home or within a place far away from you.

Peace finds you when you open the door to her. Meditation (Dhyana) originally had come from Hinduism. The earliest evidence of meditation dates back to around 1500 BC. The Vedas, a Hindu scripture, describes meditation. Through meditation, positive vibes are transmitted from the mind, body, and soul. Meditation is where you find complete liberation from all worldly objects. You learn to let go of all the negativities around you and focus only on the positive vibrations. Earth, water, sun, air, and space are the elements to awaken your inner soul and convert your wisdom into your guidance through your devotion.

After years of meditating, I found out meditation for me is a journey through peace and serenity, through time and place, and through positivity. How one person meditates has been a question even gurus cannot agree upon as it is different for each person. It is your personal journey through your awakening wisdom. A peaceful shower could be your meditation session for as you cleanse your body, you clean your inner self and awaken within the positive vibes.

Here for me, meditation was finding peace and serenity by finding an unknown connection to this place where I had not been but have a connection with. Finding no attachments, yet I found my inner love awaken to this land. I found peace within my inner soul, within a faraway land, the Netherlands.

As I had stood by the pier at the Scheveningen beach, I felt an amazing serenity as if I have come home. With the Earth beneath my feet, water from the North Sea touching my feet, the sun shining above my head, the wind blowing fresh air upon my face, and the space uniting all of this, I knew I had awakened from within. This was my journey through peace and serenity, and my meditation course was complete. I had researched why I felt like this and found out even many years ago, people had traveled to this beach as they too believed the North Sea had healing powers.

I have traveled through India, through the Ganges, and through the Caribbean Sea. I have traveled through the Atlantic Ocean and through the Pacific Ocean. I have traveled to mountain tops to find peace and live within the foothills of Mount Rainier, one of the most dangerous volcanoes in the United States. I had found satisfaction, but not peace as I knew something was missing. It is like the different forms of meditation that exist within this world, yet one must find the perfect course for him or herself.

As I found this land calling me, I found a way to travel to this land of William the Silent. As I spoke about in my other books, I had seen within my dreams the Founding Father asking me to visit. I had also seen the Prime Minister Mark Rutte come within my dreams to give me a hint about this country. So, I, the traveler, found within my journey of life a land which had completed my meditation.

As I stood within this country, I realized meditation is but what the mind, body, and soul seek and find peace within. A traveler taking the train home actually could meditate within a crowd of people. When a traveler is sitting on top of the Himalayas, the traveler might still not find peace within him or herself.

While I traveled through this amazing country, I lived amongst the past souls like William the Silent as I had walked within the New Church in Delft. I had taken boat trips with the past, present, and future through the stories told and retold by the tour guides. These tour guides shall share the same stories with you too and more as time goes on.

Through this land, I found out how much I love the past and the amazing stories left behind to guide us. I listened to stories of the witches being weighed in Oudewater. Through the tulip fields, you can see how romantic stories were written and shall be written throughout time.

From Amsterdam's Dam Square to the Binnenhof in The Hague, through the New Church in Delft, within the sands of Hook of Holland, I found this small European country a meditation ground for all souls. The country is liberal, and they accept all different race, color, and religion within one home of Orange.

All humans from different houses can travel within this country and feel at home. A woman like myself had safely traveled throughout this land and never had I felt uncomfortable or unsafe. I never had language barrier issues like I usually do while traveling in other countries, as most of the Dutch know English even though it is not their native tongue.

As a vegetarian, I had so many options to choose from. Even though most of the menus were in Dutch, the waiters and waitresses either translated the menu items or brought an English menu for me. The general public was always there trying to help me with anything I had needed. The hugs given by the Dutch are missed but shall always remain in my memories. Time shall pass and we the present shall have a bridge of separation with the future generations. Yet through the pages of my book, these memories shall live on eternally. The colorful wooden houses, the windmills, and the love stories that blossom within the flowering fields are all my gifts I have brought back with me.

Why should you travel to this country? If not for peace, serenity, and meditation, then for leisure and vacation. This country has the happiest people in this world. Go visit them and find out why this is so. See how you can incorporate the Dutch culture within your lifestyle. The children and the adults all will find this country as a blessed place to visit. This land shall be there as guidance for all of your future generations.

Adopt a healthy lifestyle and learn to ride a bike. Save this Earth by reducing pollution. Bake fresh bread and share all the secrets of baking bread with your neighbors. Unite all around a table with bread and cheese. Layer bread with cheese for a simple and quick, no fuss lunch like the Dutch. Place some sprinkles on your bread in the morning and let the day be a sprinkle of hope. Be honest like the

Dutch and when and where there is no hidden pain, see how happy you and your family become. Learn to raise your children equally and watch your children become the happiest children in the world.

From this nation, learn how they live close to work, so they can walk or bike, become healthier, get more sleep, and have a better life. Teachers should travel to this country and find out how the teachers of this country are also helping raise the children. They do not send the children back home with a ton of homework, but they send back home a happy child who can spend the rest of his or her day with happy parents.

Without any homework, the children are more productive at school. After coming home, they are not stressed about school and have time for more extracurricular activities. They do not come home with huge bags of homework and do not need parents to write a letter of excuse why their children could not finish their homework. The office workers do not stay at work and hope for overtime benefits, as the Dutch finish their jobs efficiently within work hours, without having to take time out of the family hours.

The elderly and the young are all taken care of as the Dutch have a very affordable healthcare system. The public is covered under the healthcare system and I know they must pay, but it is really affordable and easy. Life is a lesson learned for the travelers as we take the journey for ourselves and all others who too are following our footsteps on the invisible path of life. Place your own footsteps and write your own destination as you travel. Let us the past travelers be there as your guide.

Take a journey through this magical land and awaken as the happiest people on this Earth. Let the magical windmills, and the romantic tulip fields take you through the blessed grounds as you walk within the colorful wooden houses, sail within the canals in canoes, and be within the company of wonderful history as the Founding Father watches over you. Take the memories home with you as you become the inspiration for the future travelers. Let this land be your inspiration throughout time as you awaken with a blessed feeling.

The Netherlands is the magical land, where all children are protected under the umbrella of the blessed orange tree. This tree gives branches to create a canoe, to keep all the children safe within it. The children of this land

163

have united and within their hands, they too hold on to this canoe throughout all the storms of life.

Sailing around the world, spreading flowers of hope, are the citizens of this land as they share their peace, love, and joy with you the citizens of this world. Do share your peace, love, and joy with them as you too learn from them. As you plant a bed of tulips within your land, know this is the gift from another land that accepts you as a guest.

Throughout my journey, I had kept pages of memories alive within my journal of memories. One such note was, why I had found peace in the Netherlands, as I have traveled throughout this world searching for this friend of mine, known to all of you as Peace. Some questions have no answers, such as why do I love the Netherlands?

I traveled through this land and the question still came to my mind, "But why?" I thought of the Peace Palace and the International Court of Justice, which are known as temples for peace and justice. As I landed upon this conclusion chapter, I thought, "But why did the Peace Palace take birth within the Netherlands? Why is The Hague, known as 'the international city of peace and justice'?"

We the humans have our inner temples hidden within our mind, body, and soul. As we find our temples first, peace and justice shall come on their own. I found my inner temple within a land where I felt peace and justice. I call this land, *The Netherlands: Land Of My Dreams*.

Through the eyes of this traveler, my Heaven on Earth is the Netherlands as she is the land of my dreams. I hope all whom have turned the pages have also traveled through my pen and paper. Travelers we all are, taking a journey through life. Memories we leave behind are also the same memories that keep us going through the present, the future, and keep the past alive. Here as I end my book, I want to leave you with another poem I have written for the blessed land and the blessed sea.

THE NORTH SEA MEETS
THE NETHERLANDS

Through the land of my dreams, you flow.

Carrying the power of healing, you glow.

Land after land, you travel,

As the traveler you are.

My footsteps on the sand are washed away,

As you rinse them with your tears,

Yet you store my salty tears within your chest.

Time flies by,

Tides wash by,

Yet you flow throughout time and tide.

For me, today you are there.

For the traveler,

Tomorrow, you shall be there.

I cannot hold on to you,

Even though I tried,

Yet you held on to me as I floated upon your chest.

May my memories be there within your chest,

As I treasure your memories,

Throughout my journeys.

You are the traveler,

I learn from.

Our journeys merge

As I land upon your shore, where

THE NORTH SEA MEETS

THE NETHERLANDS.

Here, I leave you with a quote from an honorable King,

"I want to be a traditional king first and foremost, building on the tradition of my predecessors standing for continuity and stability in this country, but also a 21st century king who can unite, represent and encourage society."

-King Willem-Alexander of the Netherlands

ABOUT THE AUTHOR

I have lived the struggles, overcame the obstacles, as I have endured the pain and joy of life as they landed upon my door.

I like to be the unknown face to whom all can relate. I want you to see your face in the mirror when you search for me, not mine. For if it is my face in the mirror, then my friend you see a stranger. The unknown face is there so you see only yourself, your struggles, your achievements as you cross the journey of life. I want to be the face of a white, black, and brown, as well as the love we are always searching eternally for.

If this world would have allowed, I would have distributed all of my books, to you with my own hands as a gift and a message from a friend. I have taken pen to paper to spread peace throughout this Earth. My sacred soul has found peace within herself. May I through my words bring peace and solace within your soul.

You have my name and know I will always be there for anyone who seeks me. My home is Washington State, USA, yet I travel all around the world to find you, the human with humanity. Aside from my books, I love writing openly on my blog. Through this blog journey, I am available to all throughout this world. Come, let us journey together and spread positivity, as I take you on a positive journey through my blog.

For more information about any one of my books, or to read my blog posts, subscribe to my blog on my website, www.annmarieruby.com. Follow me on social media, @AnnahMariahRuby on Twitter, @TheAnnMarieRuby on

Facebook,   @ann_marie_ruby   on   Instagram,   and
@TheAnnMarieRuby on Pinterest.

BOOKS BY THE AUTHOR

I have published four books of original inspirational quotations:

Spiritual Travelers:
Life's Journey From The Past To The Present
For The Future

Spiritual Messages:
From A Bottle

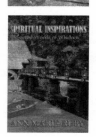

Spiritual Journey:
Life's Eternal Blessings

Spiritual Inspirations:
Sacred Words Of Wisdom

For all of you whom have requested my complete inspirational quotations, I have my complete ark of inspiration, I but call:

Spiritual Ark:
The Enchanted Journey Of Timeless Quotations

170

Do you believe in dreams? For within each individual dream, there is a hidden message and a miracle interlinked. Learn the spiritual, scientific, religious, and philosophical aspects of dreams. Walk with me as you travel through forty nights, through the pages of my book:

Spiritual Lighthouse:
The Dream Diaries Of Ann Marie Ruby

When there was no hope, I found hope within these sacred words of prayers, I but call songs. Within this book, I have for you, 100 very sacred prayers:

Spiritual Songs:
Letters From My Chest

Prayers are but the sacred doors to an individual's enlightenment. This book has 123 prayers for all humans with humanity:

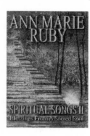

Spiritual Songs II:
Blessings From A Sacred Soul

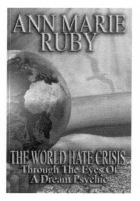

Humans have walked into an age where humanity now is being questioned as hate crimes have reached a catastrophic amount. Let us in union stop this crisis. Pick up my book and see if you too could join me in this fight:

The World Hate Crisis: Through The Eyes Of A Dream Psychic

Travel with me through the doors of birth, death, reincarnation, true soulmates, dreams, miracles, end of time, and the:

Eternal Truth: The Tunnel Of Light

Oh the sacred travelers, be like the mystical river and journey through this blessed land through my book. Be the flying bird of wisdom and learn about a land I call, Heaven on Earth. For you the traveler, this is:

The Netherlands: Land Of My Dreams

BIBLIOGRAPHY

"Cycling for All." Union Cycliste International. Web. 4
    July 2019. <https://www.uci.org/cycling-for-all/bike-
    city-label/about-bike-city-label>.

Frank, Anne. *Anne Frank: The Diary Of A Young Girl*.
    New York: Bantam, 1993.

Gregorian, Vartan. "Built to Last." *Carnegie Reporter*, vol.
    11. no. 1, Winter 2019, pp. 2-6. Web. 16 June 2019.
    <https://www.carnegie.org/media/filer_public/ad/2d/a
    d2d3ebd-e52c-494a-ba41-60378f437b4a/carnegie_
    reporter_winter_2019.pdf>.

Helliwell, J., Layard, R., & Sachs, J. World Happiness
    Report 2019. New York: Sustainable Development
    Solutions Network, 2019.

"History." *Royal House of the Netherlands*. Web. 7 July
    2019. <https://www.royal-house.nl/topics/themes/
    history>.

Jung, C. G. *The Red Book: Liber Novus*. Translated by
    Mark Kyburz, John Peck, and Sonu Shamdasani,
    Norton, 2009.

Ovink, Henk. "How Dutch Stormwater Management
    Could Have Mitigated Damage From Hurricane
    Florence." Interview by Bill Whitaker. *60 Minutes*.

CBS. 23 Sept. 2018. Web. 16 June 2019. <https://
www.cbsnews.com/news/storm-water-management-
dutch-solution-henk-ovink-hurricane-florence-
damage-60-minutes/>.

Oxfam. "The Food Index." *OxFam International*. Web. 30
June 2019. <https://www.oxfam.org.uk/what-we-
do/good-enough-to-eat>.

"Premiers-Minister Presidenten – Nederland." *Geni.com*.
Web. 16 July 2019. <https://www.geni.com/projects/
Premiers-Minister-Presidenten-Nederland/11795>.

UNICEF Office of Research. "Child Well-being in Rich
Countries: A comparative overview," *Innocenti
Report Card 11*. Florence: 2013.

"Willem-Alexander of the Netherlands Quotes."
BrainyQuote.com. BrainyMedia Inc, 2019. 3 July
2019. <https://www.brainyquote.com/quotes/
willemalexander_of_the_n_545836>.

"William the Silent." AZQuotes.com. Wind and Fly LTD,
2019. Web. 29 June 2019.
<https://www.azquotes.com/quote/1111567>

World Bank. "GDP (current US$)." The World Bank
Group. 2017. Web. 23 June 2019.
<http://data.worldbank.org/indicator/NY.GDP.MKTP
.CD?locations=NL&most_recent_value_desc=true>.

Made in the USA
Middletown, DE
09 August 2022